Praise for  The Protec

"*The Protective Circle* anyone involved in d receiving executive protection. It's a terrific optimization of Christian's first two books with critical NEW updates and additional material. The content in this book plays an important, unique role in the industry - teaching people how to start, fix, and run professional executive protection programs. These important concepts are delivered in a streamlined format that helps readers actually use and implement them. Christian has always had uncanny passion and intuition about protecting people. *The Protective Circle* is a masterclass I consider to be required reading for anyone in, or thinking of joining, the executive protection industry."

— Brian Jantzen, Strategic Advisor, Builder, Coach, Co-author of *Corporate Executive Protection* and *Public Figures, Private Lives*

"From a new EP manager in a corporate setting to an experienced Security Professional, there's a lot to learn here regardless of your background. Practicing the principles identified in *The Protective Circle* will give you a competitive advantage over others who think EP is nothing more than being a 'bodyguard.'

"*The Protective Circle* professionalizes the EP industry and gives you recognition as an expert. As expected from Christian, all the elements of professional EP are here for you to embrace and understand. Assess your EP knowledge before and after reading *The Protective Circle* to mark the growth it entails. You may wonder,

How do I sell this to the principal or to company management? Don't worry, it's all here."

— Ray O'Hara, Protection Professional

"When we entered the US market in 2017, our primary concerns were understanding the industry landscape and identifying the influencers driving the success of the top EP teams. *The Protective Circle* is a comprehensive guide to everything we wish we had known at the outset. It demystifies the industry's workings and illustrates how its various components interconnect. I highly recommend *The Protective Circle* to any agent aspiring to leadership and entrepreneurs aiming to enter the Executive Protection industry. It offers invaluable insights that will save readers time and effort by elucidating the framework behind the country's most effective EP teams."

— Pablo Ortiz-Monasterio, Founder of AS3 Driver Training

The Protective Circle

A Comprehensive Framework for Executive Protection Excellence

by Christian West

Published by How2Conquer
Atlanta, Georgia
www.how2conquer.com

How2Conquer is an imprint of White Deer Publishing, LLC
www.whitedeerpublishing.net

First edition, March 2024
Ebook edition created 2024

Illustrations and cover design by Telia Garner
Edited by Lauren Kelliher, Terry Dunne, Charlotte Bleau

Library of Congress Cataloging-in-Publication Data is on file at the Library of Congress, Washington, DC.

Print ISBN 978-1-945783-26-5
Ebook ISBN 978-1-945783-35-7

For information about special discounts available for bulk purchases, contact How2Conquer special sales www.how2conquer.com/bulk-orders

Contents

Contents

 INTRODUCTION:

The Foundations of Quality in Executive Protection

The executive protection industry is rapidly expanding, driven by the growing demand for personal security in an increasingly complex and uncertain world. However, despite the industry's growth in size, number of programs, and professionalization, there still exist many misconceptions about the contemporary practice of executive protection.

For one thing, we still run into many people who associate high-end personal protection with stereotypical perceptions of either the US Secret Service or more-brawn-than-brain bodyguards with a penchant for punching paparazzi. For another, even industry insiders don't always agree on what constitutes good personal protection, which qualifications and certifications should be mandatory for agents and managers, or what distinguishes the best programs from the second best. This lack of standardization and consensus on evidence-based best practices hinders the industry's ability to establish clear benchmarks for excellence. It also perpetuates many misunderstandings between clients and providers, within the corporations and family offices that are the biggest users of our services, and even among the people who are the backbone of the industry.

In *The Protective Circle*, I aim to address these mis-comprehensions by digging into what I perceive to be the fundamentals of quality in executive protection and presenting these as straightforwardly as possible. Drawing on more than 30 years of experience working with some of the largest and most complex executive protection programs in the world, *The Protective Circle* aims to establish a common frame of reference for protective excellence for a wide range of executive protection stakeholders on both sides of the customer/provider divide.

Among customers, two main target groups emerge: family offices and corporations. Different as they are, within both these types of organizations a range of stakeholders play similar and crucial roles in enabling good protection. These always include the principal who requires protection, of course, as well as executive assistants responsible for planning and scheduling the principal's time. They might also include Chief Security Officers (CSOs) or other C-suite players that influence the frames that define the protective program, as well as many other individuals working in security and risk management roles. Procurement personnel responsible for vendor selection should also find *The Protective Circle* helpful.

On the provider side, the book is aimed at anyone seeking to deliver quality executive protection services. Whether they're owners, directors, managers, team leads, or the agents providing the day-to-day protection, *The Protective Circle* is intended to offer insights and guidance for all levels of involvement in the hope that they'll be able to use some of its ideas to up their own game.

I'm here to share what I've learned so far. Some of this experience comes from running very large programs; some derives from working with much smaller clients. I gained much of this experience by founding and operating two successful executive protection companies including AS Solution, which was one of the largest private executive protection companies globally at the time of its sale in 2017. I've worked with exceptional companies, vendors, and individuals. I've also encountered less impressive counterparts. All of this experience has formed my understanding of what distinguishes good executive protection from mediocre practices.

In *The Protective Circle*, I aim to introduce new concepts and perspectives that build upon the foundations laid in my two previous books. In that connection, I wish to acknowledge the invaluable contributions of a few people. First, thanks to Brian Jantzen, a long-time collaborator who has provided unique insights into executing and managing good executive protection programs. Brian co-authored my first book, *Corporate Executive Protection: An Introduction for Corporations and Security Professionals*, and my second book, *Public Figures, Private Lives: An Introduction to Protective Security for High Net Worth Individuals and Family Offices*. I would also like to extend my gratitude to Ivor Terret and Jared Van Driessche, two professionals with whom I've also worked for years, who helped write my second book.

Why write this third book now? After selling AS Solution and undergoing a few subsequent mergers, I decided it was time to take a break from more than 300 travel days per year. During this hiatus, I pursued my passion for developing talent and established a company providing online training solutions — a learning alternative I believe the industry lacked. As I reflected on my future endeavors, I recognized the need for a renewed focus on enhancing the *quality* of executive protection services. With this in mind, I began digging into the core drivers of protective excellence and the contours of *The Protective Circle* began to take shape.

The Protective Circle represents my current thinking on what constitutes quality executive protection. Keeping what still works from my first two books and endeavoring to further distill the essence of good protection, I've integrated a few basic but powerful ideas that I hope will help dispel persistent misconceptions of executive protection for corporations and family offices and contribute to moving the industry forward.

These three core drivers of protective excellence will be familiar to many. Some will consider them obvious or even banal. That's fine with me — as long as these quality drivers continue to inform protective programs regardless of their size and budget, and as long as they work together in an integrated way. Here they are:

1. **Quality executive protection is risk-based:** At its core, executive protection is a personalized form of risk management. Understanding how to assess and mitigate the specific personal security risks our principals face is crucial to designing and implementing quality programs. The first chapter invites readers to understand executive protection within the broader context of risk management, and why ongoing and proactive updates of the threats and vulnerabilities that constitute personal risk should always dynamically inform executive protection programs.

2. **Quality executive protection is comprehensive:** Excellence in executive protection requires a holistic, 360-degree approach that covers all aspects of personal security, not just the most obvious ones or the ones we know from popular media. To clarify the importance of this

comprehensiveness, I introduce a new framework, the Protective Circle™, a model that explains the importance of holistic thinking regarding not only our principals' varied (and often misunderstood) security needs, but also the multiple categories of threats and vulnerabilities they typically face — and the protective capabilities required to mitigate the resulting risks. I've found that the Protective Circle is a simple way to make clear to all kinds of stakeholders what executive protection is, how it works, and why it works best when approached comprehensively. It's also a helpful tool for planning new protective programs and evaluating or improving existing ones.

3. Good executive protection relies on well-trained personnel: As I've said many times before, executive protection is a people business. Excellence in executive protection is always a synergy between highly trained professionals, efficient processes, and cutting-edge technology. But it all starts with good people who have good training. That's why I include chapters that dig into both the hard and soft skills that executive protection professionals must master, how these capabilities play a role in the Protective Circle, and why training must always be a priority for successful programs.

These core quality drivers are interdependent. You can't provide quality protection by choosing just one or two of them — you need all three. Good programs are good because providers continue to appreciate these quality drivers as they build and maintain protective programs across changing locations and times, and even when no one's looking.

I'll delve into these drivers and examine their inter-relatedness in various ways in the coming chapters, but I also explore numerous other facets of good executive protection. I invite you to embark on this journey with me as I try to make clear what constitutes quality executive protection and seek to further professionalize the industry. Your feedback, comments, questions, and suggestions are highly valued as we work together to enable more excellence in executive protection.

Enjoy the book!

— **Christian West**

SECTION 1:

Necessity, Nature, and Scope of Executive Protection Programs

The last thing Bob wanted was executive protection.

Bob never really wanted to be extremely wealthy. Things just worked out that way, as they sometimes do with talented entrepreneurs. He was highly intelligent, creative, and crazy about coding. He had a good idea, and the timing was right. If you asked Bob, he'd say he got lucky. The real geniuses aren't usually the ones who claim to be smart.

As the founder of what would become a highly successful startup and then a major corporation, Bob worked hard and often. Still, he found time to pursue other interests like riding his mountain bike, cooking, and hanging out with friends. Despite the ever-growing valuations of his company, he considered himself to be a "regular Joe" and disdained what he considered to be the affectations of the super-rich: drivers, personal chefs, security, and all the rest.

The money piled in, and Bob felt good sharing it. He donated to charities and would walk down the street handing out $100 bills to unhoused people. There were thousands of unhoused people in his city, and while he knew he couldn't help all of them, passing out some C-notes every once in a while seemed the least he could do.

Soon enough, word of the guy with lots of money spread on the street. Crowds of people would gather when Bob was around. He began to be recognized almost everywhere he went, and people seemed to like to interact with him — for their own reasons, of course. After someone got ahold of his cell phone number, Bob started to get calls from strangers. At first only a few, then many. Most of the calls had to do with requests for money and favors; others offered unwanted business advice; some were antagonistic; none made him feel any better.

Bob didn't enjoy the incessant attention. In fact, it made him uneasy and eventually anxious. He changed his phone number and stopped handing out cash on the street. But the level of public scrutiny only grew as his company went from success to success, his personal wealth skyrocketed, and the media shined an ever-larger spotlight on him.

Calls came in from obscure "friends" and acquaintances. His company's HR department began to require background checks and screenings for new employees. Unsolicited investment opportunities poured in. Lawyers started talking about liabilities that Bob had never imagined; now he had to protect himself from them. How was he suddenly responsible for so many potential mishaps?

Bob had been exposed to security at corporate events but wanted nothing to do with it in his private life. For one thing, he didn't think he was special enough for any bad actors to be particularly interested in him. For another, who wanted all those goonish-looking bodyguards around? He'd seen his share of news reports about celebrity bodyguards punching photographers and thought both sides of the fight were idiots. Maybe the whole scene with burly guys in black suits, dark sunglasses, and squiggly earpieces worked for the president, but Bob didn't even own a suit and wouldn't be caught dead in a blacked-out Suburban. He enjoyed his lifestyle and didn't want to be encumbered by worries about his safety or any extra security measures.

Still, when he built a new home, he agreed to his company's and contractor's advice that the building site get some guards. Leaving the building site and increasingly valuable fixtures unwatched at night was a risk the contractor didn't want to take, and he couldn't have his own tradespeople stay there 24/7. What began as a guy guarding the construction site eventually became full-time residential security. Bob's wife didn't want to deal with all the strangers knocking on the door of their new home; she sometimes felt unsafe when he was away and didn't want the kids to notice anything.

Business was good, valuations were even better. After a while, Bob wasn't just rich but super rich and very well known. His company was often in the press, and although he didn't look for controversy, his views became news. He couldn't go anywhere without being recognized. Even when he was riding a bike, people had no hesitation in chatting him up and slowing him down. He could be accosted on the street and challenged publicly for almost anything — even in front of his young children.

That was the turning point in terms of his perception of personal security: He'd become so prominent that he could no longer get away with being the regular Joe that he still felt like and wanted to be. He and his family were fair game to strangers, passersby, and eccentrics. He hadn't wanted any security because he felt it would put a crimp in his lifestyle, but all the unwanted attention and attendant hassles were having an even bigger impact on how he wanted to live.

Bob's growing company had recently hired a security director whose main responsibilities were the physical security of their headquarters and other offices. He had experience with things like biometric access control, guards, and contingency plans for earthquakes and fires, but not with personal protection. At the suggestion of a board member, the CFO asked the security director to look into what other similar companies did in terms of executive protection. She wanted him to benchmark with similar CEOs in similar companies: What kinds of programs did they run, how were they organized, and what did they cost?

The security director had worked at a few larger companies and had a good network, so he called a few other security directors and CSOs to get a lay of the land. It turned out that benchmarking personal protection wasn't as straight-forward as the CFO had hoped. One of the benchmarked CEOs was richer than God; another ran a pharma company that was constantly in the news; a third had political views that brought the trolls out of their caves and kept social media servers humming. Nonetheless, the benchmarking exercise was helpful and gave the CFO and board a better overview of their situation and options.

Not long after, Bob's company began requiring he have close protection — initially at public events and when he traveled to high-risk countries, then more and more. As time went on and both his company's and his own prominence grew, Bob's executive protection coverage became the rule rather than the exception. It expanded to wherever he traveled, including the commute to and from work, and to his family as well.

Chapter 1-1:

Executive protection is risk management made personal

Executive protection is admittedly new to many people. And like Bob, they often have negative preconceptions of it. At its core, however, executive protection is just another form of risk management, something that most organizations deal with every day.

Corporations and family offices are used to dealing with risk at a strategic level. Under the oversight of boards of directors, chief risk officers (CROs) are tasked with managing a variety of risks that can have a major impact on assets and earnings, including risks that are competitive, financial, operational, political, regulatory, reputational, and technological. However, far fewer organizations are accustomed to managing personal risk in a strategic way.

This chapter looks at executive protection through the lens of risk management. The benefits of this exercise are double-edged: It helps demystify what might seem unknown and strange to some principals and organizations, and it provides a time-tested framework to better understand how the many moving parts of executive protection come together to mitigate risk at a personal level.

Defining Risk

The Oxford Dictionary definition of risk is "a situation involving exposure to danger; the possibility that something unpleasant will happen." This is accurate enough for most situations, but in the protection industry, we like to break risk into its two constituent parts — threats and vulnerabilities — to arrive at a more precise definition of risk that I'll use and refer to many times throughout *The Protective Circle*:

Risks are where threats and vulnerabilities intersect to harm the principal. Risks are the potential for harm (loss, damage, etc.) to the principal that arise when threats exploit or circumvent vulnerabilities. Risks cannot be completely eliminated, but they can be managed and mitigated. In executive protection, risk management involves identifying, evaluating, and prioritizing risks to the principal according to probability and impact — and designing and implementing protective programs that reduce their probability and impact.

Threats are the dangers we protect the principal against. Threats are the bad things (and/or people, events, circumstances, etc.) that might or could cause harm to the principal. These bad things could be intentional or unintentional, probable or improbable, and have major or minor consequences. Protectors can't necessarily control or manage threats, but they can become aware of them, evaluate them, and make plans to protect against them.

Vulnerabilities are the ways threats reach the principal. Vulnerabilities are weaknesses in protective programs — or gaps in the Protective Circle — that can be exploited or otherwise surpassed, so threats can reach and harm the principal. Much of what protectors do concerns the control and management of discernible vulnerabilities to predictable threats.

Before getting into the types of threats and vulnerabilities most relevant for the mitigation of personal risk, let's remember the most successful personal protection programs have their limitations, too.

There Is No Absolute Security: the Difference between Risk Mitigation and Risk Elimination

Even a person barricaded 24/7 in a concrete safe room beneath Fort Knox faces some risk and cannot be said to be completely secure. To start with the obvious, everyone is going to die, and no one knows exactly when that'll be or exactly what else the future will bring. Sorry, I don't make the rules.

Moving to the slightly less obvious, unless they're the top dog of a superpower like the USA, China, or Russia, executive protection principals can almost always find someone with "better" security than their own. Of course, they can find far more people whose personal security is worse than theirs, too.

Less obvious again is what could be called the premise and promise of professional executive protection: The best personal security isn't the one that will keep the principal alive no matter what — it's the personal security that mitigates risk effectively and is sustainable because the principal is willing to live with it.

Sustainably successful security strikes an acceptable balance between the benefits of risk mitigation and the personal and financial costs of protection. No matter who you are or what your situation is, you can practically always improve security if you're willing to restrict personal freedom or use additional resources to mitigate more risks, regardless of how unlikely those risks might be. However, very few people want to spend their entire lives in the security of an impenetrable bunker just because that's the safest place for them to be.

Principles of Risk Management

There are many risk management models, but they all boil down to a similar process. Most of these models comprise four processes, i.e., steps two to five of the diagram shown below. As you'll see, I believe the risk-governance process is a necessary addition to the traditional model.

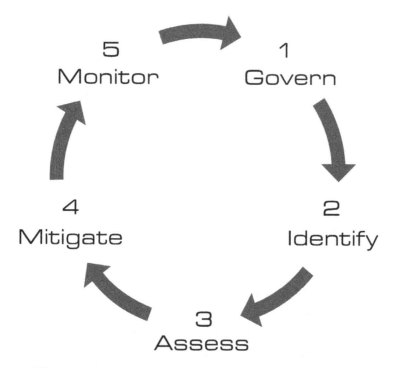

First, understand how to deal with risk **governance**, or how risk management relates to an organi-zation's control frameworks, management processes, culture, and leadership.

Then, **identify** the risks that matter, i.e., those that are potentially problematic and deserve to be analyzed. How can you hope to mitigate risks that haven't been recognized and classified?

The next step is **risk assessment or evaluation**, understanding the components of risk as well as risks' potential impact and probability — and ultimately prioritizing the risks that require resources to mitigate.

Apply that understanding to **mitigate** — take action to eliminate, or more realistically, reduce identified and assessed risks to acceptable levels.

Finally, **monitor** risks and risk management activities. Are objectives met or not? Is communication flowing optimally? Do risk identification, assessment, and control processes need to be updated?

And then, the whole process starts over again and keeps on rolling. Hopefully, more and more effectively and efficiently than the last time.

Step 1: Risk governance and executive protection - it's complicated

Many models of the risk mitigation process skip this initial step and go right into risk identification. Most everyone in the executive protection industry does the same. Even large corporations with well-established risk management and governance procedures often neglect to govern personal security risks with the same consideration they'd give other risk categories, such as currency exchange rates or supply chain disruptions.

Why would CROs or their boards of directors waste time on executive protection when they have other, bigger, riskier fish to fry? Why should executive protection teams care about risk governance when this is a) kind of fluffy, b) way above our pay level, and c) not anything we can influence, anyway? It's because poor risk governance is often a root cause of failed executive protection programs, and failed programs can have significant negative consequences.

Risk governance as it relates to executive protection is hard for many organizations to get a handle on because it falls outside the risk governance structures they normally use. For one thing, corporate oversight of personal risk is often poor. Corporate decision-makers rarely understand the components of personal risk; nor do they commonly benchmark personal risk management against that of other corporations. For another, personal risks can at the same time be considered both individual and company-wide. Although the principal and their family are the ones most concerned with the principal's personal safety, the impact of the risk might have repercussions throughout the company. Indeed, that's why many such corporate programs are board-mandated.

Responsibility for managing personal security risks can fall into a gray area between the corporation and other legal entities. Consider, for example, a principal who requires 24/7 protection and on any given day might be occupied with decisions regarding a corporation, a family office, an NGO, and personal concerns. Which entity should govern risk, and who should pay for which risk mitigation services?

The personal nature of executive protection has other potential consequences for risk governance. For example, if the principal (or their significant other) is unhappy with the performance of the protective team, then risk mitigation may stop at a moment's notice and without any kind of involvement from those normally concerned with corporate risk governance. It happens.

To understand personal risk governance as it relates to executive protection in organizational contexts, I introduce the **risk management stakeholder matrix** (see page 20). The matrix presents an overview of the various stakeholders that can and do impact decisions regarding personal security programs in corporations and family offices.

Note that this example is descriptive, not prescriptive: I'm not here to tell corporations or family offices how they should manage risk; rather, I'm describing how governance of a hypothetical personal security risk might look from a provider's point of view. Others might add or subtract stakeholders or rate their relative influence differently, and that's fine. For the sake of example, I've taken the liberty of populating the matrix according to my own experience, but there's plenty of room to wriggle and quibble with how I scored the stakeholders listed.

While imperfect, the matrix is useful in at least three ways:

1. **The matrix can be used to identify disconnects between those who experience, govern, and mitigate personal risk in complex organizations.**
   For example, it's important to note:

   - The ownership of personal risk is often imprecise and more opaque than other risk categories that corporations typically deal with.
   - The influencers of personal risk mitigation, coverage levels, and budgets are often numerous and unexpected.
   - Corporate protection employees and primary vendor employees wield similar degrees of influence on risk governance, i.e., not much.

2. **The matrix can help assess and clarify what has and could go wrong in protective program governance.**
   Retroactively, the matrix can help diagnose personal risk governance mistakes and failures — and inform improved governance practices.
   Proactively, for example, in connection with RFP rounds with vendors, the matrix can be a useful way to clarify risk governance and its consequences for protective programs.

STAKEHOLDERS		Who governs the prinicpal's risk management?
Protectee(s)	The principal	(Sometimes/to some extent)
	The principal's spouse/significant other	(Never)
	Other members of the principal's family	(Never)
Corporate/ family office/ngo decision makers	Board of directors	(Usually/always)
	The principal's executive assistant	(Never)
	Chief risk officer	(Usually/always)
	Chief security officer	(Usually/always)
	Chief financial officer	(Usually/always)
Own protection employees	Executive protection manager	(Sometimes/to some extent)
	Executive protection supervisor	(Never)
	Executive protection agents	(Never)
Primary protection vendor employees	Executive protection manager	(Sometimes/to some extent)
	Executive protection supervisor	(Never)
	Executive protection agents, drivers, others	(Never)
Other protection vendor employees	Secondary executive protection agents, drivers, others	(Never)
	Tertiary executive protection agents, drivers, others	(Never)

Key	Never	Rarely	Sometimes/to some extent	Usually/ always

Who influences the principal's risk management?	Who influences the principal's protective coverage levels?	Who influences the principal's protective budgets?	Who gets blamed if protection goes wrong?

3. `The matrix is helpful in benchmarking exercises.` Understanding how other organizations govern personal risk — or don't — is a good way to avoid predictable pitfalls and hone in on best practices.

Step 2: Risk identification — you can't tell the players without a scorecard

The next step in the risk management process is risk identification: Document not only what could go wrong, but also when, where, why, and how these things could go wrong and negatively affect the principal. The Protective Circle (presented in more detail in the next chapter) is a useful tool in the risk identification process.

The Protective Circle helps us identify personal security risks in two ways. First, it reminds us to consider risk as it relates to all four of the principal's basic security needs: physical, productive, reputational, and lifestyle. Then, it encourages us to break risks into their component parts, the various threats and vulnerabilities that can meet and result in harm to the principal.

Identifying the personal security risks that face the principal requires a solid understanding of security in general and of the principal's situation in particular. For example, good, all-around protective security expertise will go a long way in helping to identify the various kinds of physical attack threats that can potentially occur (e.g., a protester's pie in the face, an IED, and everything in between), and the vulnerabilities related to where and when these threats could potentially occur (e.g., while driving, walking, at home, or at work). But it requires insight into the principal's lifestyle and preferences to understand that the principal likes to run every morning (on the exact same route when at home) and what kinds of vulnerabilities that might entail.

The Protective Circle

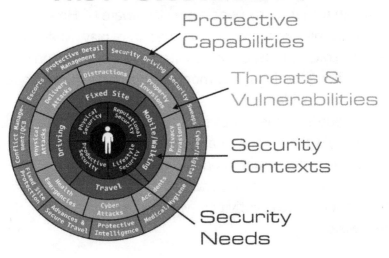

Protective
Capabilities

Threats &
Vulnerabilities

Security
Contexts

Security
Needs

Factoring in risk multipliers

The consideration of **risk multipliers** — how various aspects of risk might interact with each other to increase risks or create new ones — can be an important element of the risk identification process. As an example, let's look at how two well-known risk multipliers could affect the security of our hypothetical principal on their morning run.

Prominence is one obvious risk multiplier that impacts many executive protection principals. A highly prominent person will likely face high risk in many situations. For whatever reason (e.g., exposure in traditional and/or social media, being the figurehead of a controversial enterprise such as a fossil fuel or pharmaceutical company, or strong political views) some people are more conspicuous than others. As such, some of the risks they face are greater than those of "normal" people, and they can't necessarily do "normal" things like going for a morning run (or shopping for groceries with their children, etc.) without being recognized and increasing their risk.

Another well-known risk multiplier is **time-and-place predictability**, which makes it easier for bad actors to know when and where the principal will be. Morning running rituals are only one example of such predictability. Home-office commutes are another that many people are also aware of. However, time-and-place predictability also comes into play when A-listers step onto red carpets, CEOs speak at public events, and in many, many other situations that most people don't think about, but protection providers must.

Of course, other factors, including the principal's personal and lifestyle preferences, can also multiply risk. If the morning runs lead up to a marathon through a large city, the risk is multiplied. If rock climbing and parkour are more the principal's thing, then these activities would clearly multiply risk in other ways.

Introducing protective intelligence

When we identify and assess risks, it's important to remember that life is a movie, not a Polaroid. Like everything else, threats and vulnerabilities change constantly. Over time, unknown risks become known, and known risks disappear. The consequences of opportunistic, spontaneous threats can be just as great or greater than those of planned, premeditated threats. Does this mean that risk identification and assessment will necessarily be out of date and therefore superfluous? No. But it does mean that protective teams need to look around — and look forward — in addition to looking back.

On the one hand, some form of an agreed risk, threat, and vulnerability assessment (RTVA) should always be performed before protective programs are designed and implemented. How can we structure and build out mitigation procedures without understanding the risks the principal is facing? And how can this analysis be better than the assumptions upon which it's based?

On the other hand, however, even the most junior executive protection agent must be running an ongoing RTVA process at every moment of every shift and be ready to act on it — even though this spur-of-the-moment RTVA contradicts a more formalized and agreed upon version created months earlier. If pink elephants are charging toward the principal right now, then pink elephants are now a known threat to avoid, escape from, or confront regardless of what we thought we knew two minutes ago.

Ultimately, it's the quality of ongoing, proactive **protective intelligence** that determines the quality of risk identification and analysis processes. Clearly, protective intelligence needs to be flexible and dynamic in addition to — and not instead of — being accurate and well documented.

Step 3: Assessment – not all risks are created equal

The third step in the risk mitigation process concerns assessing the risks identified above. This is a question of evaluating the effect and probability of all risks and prioritizing the risks accordingly. While this assessment primarily concerns risks to the principal, it's often necessary or at least helpful to include members of the principal's family if the impact of a risk to them would in turn have a significant impact on the principal.

I'd love to report that assessments of personal risk probability are based on clearly defined procedures that provide objective and repeatable results. In my experience, however, these are, more or less, informed judgment calls. Whereas actuaries use a variety of sophisticated statistical models and datasets based on hundreds of thousands of people to estimate risk levels and insurance premiums, protective specialists typically rely on their experience and a population of one, the principal, to assess and prioritize his or her security risks.

With that said, a well-informed judgment call is much better than none at all because risk assessment and prioritization have important practical consequences for a range of issues, including:

- Protective program scope and design
- Budget allocations for people, procedures, and technology
- Staff capabilities and training requirements
- Program management focus and follow-up

Impact of loss

Obviously, the greatest impact of loss would be related to physical security, i.e., the death of or severe injury to the principal. However, as already stated, losses that relate to reputational, productive, and lifestyle security can also have a significant impact on the principal.

Beyond that, however, lie the interests of the company and its shareholders. That's why the corporation's board of directors typically considers a spectrum of factors when deciding whether to mandate an executive protection program for one or more of its principals.

One factor is shareholder value. If a company's reputation and competitiveness are closely associated with one or two high-profile individuals, then the company's perceived value — and actual share price — can be immediately affected if something happens to those individuals.

Duty of care is another issue. If individuals working for the corporation are exposed to personal risk as part of their jobs, then executive protection may in some cases be considered a duty of care since it could mitigate a reasonable and foreseeable risk, and failure to do so could be considered negligent.

Another potential loss, which is often overlooked, has to do with productivity. Few boards would expect a well-remunerated top executive to spend time making his or her own travel arrangements. But what about the time execs spend moving between airports, hotels, and meetings while traveling? Secure travel logistics, a key component of many executive protection programs, not only keeps executives safer while on the road, but also enables them to boost productivity by staying focused on the job rather than dealing with rental cars and taxi queues.

Similar logic may apply to daily commutes between home and the office. For example, a principal living and working in Silicon Valley might have a 15 mile (25 kilometer) commute that could take as much as 60 to 90 minutes each way, every day. If an executive protection program can help make 12 to 18 hours of the principal's time far more productive every week, the business case for including driving the principal to and from work can be quite straightforward given the differences between the hourly rates of a CEO and a professional security driver.

Probability of risk

Specific threats from persons of interest (POIs) to the principal or his or her family are typically at the top of the list and need to be identified and analyzed to keep people safe now and in the future. Understandably, such threats are often a part of the company's decision to instigate an executive protection program. However, we know from experience — and from the Secret Service's "Exceptional Case Study Project"[1] — that potential perpetrators who pose the biggest threats are rarely those who actually make direct threats. This means that assessing risk probability could entail more than recording known threats; it could also encompass proactive protective intelligence to identify unknown threats, including probable and possible persons and groups of interest in locations where the principal's presence is predictable.

For reasons that include everything from income inequality to crime rates and police salaries, the probability of opportunistic physical attacks is greater in some places than in others. An investment banker traveling to Bogotá likely faces greater risk than one going to Boston. Does that mean the banker can't get mugged in Beantown or travel to Colombia to work on a deal? No, but it does mean that the relative probability of opportunistic physical attacks should be considered when designing protective coverage.

And while we're on the topic of travel, do you know what the biggest single risk while traveling is? No, it's neither muggings, carjackings, nor terrorist attacks. It's getting hurt in a road accident while driving in a car. According to the WHO, about 1.3 million are killed worldwide in road accidents annually, with another 20 to 50 million incurring non-fatal injuries. More than 90 percent of these fatalities occur in low- and middle-income countries. Again, this doesn't mean that our principals can never travel to anywhere but high-income countries. However, the statistical probability of serious road accidents could and should have consequences for the kinds of cars and drivers that protective teams source in these places.

As mentioned above, prominence is a risk multiplier that must be considered when assessing risk probability. The more prominent an organization and its principals, the more likely they are to be approached by POIs. These interactions could range from slight to enormous invasions of privacy; they might include troublesome but largely innocuous exchanges with strangers (You're rich, I'm not; How about giving me some of your money?); they can also be outright hostile (kidnapping of the principal or his family). There are tools to evaluate the relative prominence of various principals, and these should be used in assessing the probability of risk.

Everything else being equal, some industries are more prominent than others. This, too, should be taken into consideration when assessing risk. For example, the oil and gas industry is under close scrutiny from many quarters, not all of them friendly. The number of persons, disaffected or otherwise, who take an interest in a petroleum company and its principals is likely to be higher than those who keep an eye on a food company. Until someone has a beef with the food company's products or practices, that is.

Ultimately, protective programs designed to mitigate risk should be based on some kind of risk assessment matrix that enables prioritization according to the dimensions of impact and probability. A matrix can be a good way to clarify and illustrate the relative priority of various risks (see **Risk Assessment Matrix on page 30**). To be useful, such a matrix must:

- **Achieve the right balance between generality and specificity** — so it covers relevant threats and vulnerabilities without turning into an encyclopedia.

- **Be shareable** — on a need-to-know basis, between protective program managers and relevant stakeholders in the corporation or family office, so these underlying assumptions for mitigation are made explicit and transparent.

- **Be dynamic** — as risk prioritization can change due to updated RTVAs, new business ventures, the arrival of new family members, and many other factors.

- **Be actionable** — yes, planet Earth may be hit by a devastating meteor at any moment, but rockets to deflect its path aren't something any protective agent keeps in her back pocket.

Finally, it's important to remember everything changes. New business ventures, the birth of a child, and any number of other events can easily mean that protective programs need to revisit risk assessments to stay relevant.

RISK ASSESSMENT MATRIX		IMPACT				
		NEGLIGIBLE	MINOR	MODERATE	MAJOR	CATASTROPHIC
PROBABILITY	HIGHLY LIKELY					
	LIKELY					
	POSSIBLE					
	UNLIKELY					
	HIGHLY UNLIKELY					

Key	Extreme	High	Moderate	Low

Step 4: Risk mitigation is the heart of executive protection

After identifying and assesing personal risks, ask: How do executive protection providers mitigate them to acceptable levels and in a way that's acceptable to the principal? What is acceptable? Why not just remove the risks altogether?

Let's start with the obvious, the difference between risk mitigation and risk elimination. Yes, executive protection agents (EPAs) would eliminate many risks to their principals by requiring them to never travel and to remain ensconced in a fortress of a corporate headquarters or a private residence. If they did insist on venturing out anyway, EPAs could, given enough resources, replicate the US Secret Service to escort principals wherever they go with a small army of people in black. Alternatively, hire the bulkiest bodybuilders at the gym and pay them to push people out of the principal's way. Despite the "bodyguard" stereotypes that most people have learned through the media, however, this isn't what executive protection is all about.

Good executive protection programs are designed to fit in, not stick out. They should be tailored to the principal's personal preferences and company culture, and mirror those. Of course, the reduction of identified personal risks to acceptable levels requires a good understanding of the threats and vulnerabilities described in the assessment process outlined above. However, doing it in a way that's acceptable to the principal requires understanding the principal's four personal security needs (physical, productive, reputational, lifestyle) outlined in the introduction of the Protective Circle in the next chapter, not to mention making best use of available resources and budgets.

The two-minute overview of tactical protective risk mitigation

Rather than provide the standard operating procedures (SOPs) for any protective practice, my purpose here is to clarify what good executive protection actually is and to dispel some of the myths and preconceptions that still abound.

With that proviso in mind, here's a mini version of what executive protection practitioners do — or should do — to keep principals safe, productive, and reasonably happy.
1. Prepare
2. Avoid
3. Escape
4. Confront
5. Escape

Preparation is the essential first step in executive protection

Like many others who provide some kind of protective service, executive protection practitioners know the importance of preparation. Stakeholders in client organizations must also appreciate the importance of preparedness in order to ask good questions and allocate adequate resources.

As we'll see in **Section 3: The Importance of Training**, preparation basics include suitable training and equipment. For example, principals must be able to count on agents who have a firm (and updated) grasp of first aid and are equipped with decent med kits. This has consequences for recruitment, readiness, and budgets.

Tactically, preparation comprises at least some kind of current risk evaluation and the all-important advance, where agents familiarize themselves with the places to which they will later bring the principal. Advances are a necessary part of preparedness, but unfortunately are often eliminated or squeezed because they cost time and money.

An ounce of prevention is worth a pound of black belts in Brazilian jiu-jitsu

Contrary to Hollywood myths, the best "bodyguards" are the ones who avoid conflicts, not the ones who pummel their adversaries to a pulp. They'll happily cross the street to avoid potential trouble. They'll even go around the block if that's what it takes.

Good executive protection agents and teams spend far more time avoiding and preventing conflicts than they do winning them. Friction-free movements enable principals to get from A to B efficiently and productively — and keep them and their protective teams out of harm's way (and the tabloids).

Know your escape routes — and when and how to use them

Well-trained protective agents will always run away from trouble, not at it, until escape is no longer an option. Yes, this includes dealing with paparazzi with all the charm of a swarm of locusts.

That's why their brains consistently dedicate at least some processing power to scanning for potential escape routes. If the fight-or-flight alarm starts ringing, it's far easier to flee if you have an idea of where you're going.

If you must fight, do it right . . .

Sometimes, push comes to shove. Freezing or fleeing just doesn't work, and the only recourse is confronting the threat. Well, then fight as if the principal's life depended on it, because it just might.

Here, preparedness and training are essential. Clearly, agents need to understand the use of force principles and any relevant legislation and guidelines. They will definitely need to be proficient in some kind of unarmed close-quarter combat technique. In some contexts — albeit far fewer than most people imagine — they may also need proficiency with firearms.

. . . then get back to flight

I'm not talking about a drawn-out battle here. The goal is to use as little force as possible, as quickly as possible, and then get the principal out of there.

Step 5: Monitoring risk mitigation — who's keeping the score?

It's been said many times in business that if you're not keeping score, you're only practicing. This is also true for executive protection. It's important to monitor personal risk mitigation for at least two reasons.

First, the risks principals face are constantly changing. Good teams deal with the dynamic nature of risk every day and realize that new situations could entail new threats and vulnerabilities. This doesn't require revamping the entire risk mitigation strategy once a month, of course, but it's a good idea to take a critical look at RTVAs and program setups on an annual basis. Just as corporations routinely perform SWOT exercises and update strategies for all kinds of other priorities, they also need to review and revise how they deal with executive protection.

Second, as we'll see in **Section 2: Managing the Executive Protection Program**, monitoring risk mitigation performance is an essential element of good protective program management. Clients must be able to hold suppliers to agreed standards and contracts. Providers, whether in house or outsourced, must be able to measure how well their teams meet the operational goals they set for themselves.

	Key Takeaways
1	In the context of executive protection, risk is best understood by examining its two essential parts: threats and vulnerabilities.
2	Risk management models are also useful in understanding the personal security risks that executive protection is meant to mitigate.
3	Our five-step risk management model provides a comprehensive approach to personal security risk management: **1. Risk governance** How risks to the principal relate to the organization's control frameworks, management structures, culture, etc.; introducing the risk management stakeholder matrix **2. Risk identification** Recognizing relevant risks including understanding their components (threats and vulnerabilities) and risk multipliers; the role of protective intelligence **3. Risk assessment** Evaluating risks' probability and impact, and prioritizing the most significant among them for mitigation; introducing the risk assessment matrix **4. Risk mitigation** Choosing and implementing the proper means to reduce risks to acceptable levels **5. Risk monitoring** Ongoing surveillance of risks and risk-mitigation activities
4	Protection professionals tactically mitigate security risks through processes of preparation, avoidance, escape, confrontation, and escape (again).

Chapter 1-2:

The Protective Circle — a comprehensive approach to mitigating personal security risks

Security is best when it deals with risk comprehensively and leaves as few protective gaps as possible. This 360-degree approach to risk has proven its worth in countless situations throughout history and is valid whether we're talking about personal, cyber, national, or any other kind of security.

The circle is an apt metaphor for protection. Roman legionaries formed "orbis" to defend against superior forces. Moats surround castles. Pioneers circled their wagons against attack. But it's the completeness of the form that matters, not the basic shape. The key concept here is plugging the principal's vulnerabilities to threats in a comprehensive way: We want to lock the back door as well as the front door, and all the windows, too.

In executive protection, good security is comprehensive in multiple ways. It starts with a multifaceted understanding of the principal's basic security needs. It takes into consideration the multiple activities and places in which the principal spends time and the various vulnerabilities to threats that may be associated with those times and places. It considers a broad range of threats, some of which are more predictable than others. It evaluates risk based on assessments of the identified threats and vulnerabilities. And it relies on a wide spectrum of protective capabilities to mitigate those risks.

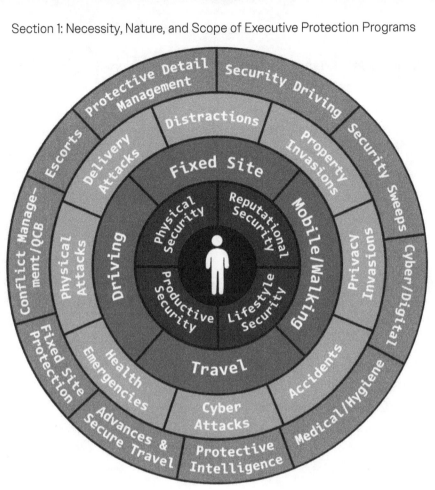

Introducing the Protective Circle

The Protective Circle is a model that represents the comprehensive nature of quality executive protection programs. Each ring represents a different program dimension, and the various ring segments represent different categories of that dimension. As we'll see throughout this section and beyond, the Protective Circle can be used in at least three ways.

First, we've found the Protective Circle extremely helpful in explaining to stakeholders new to the field what good executive protection is all about — and more than placing a few beefy guys in black suits near the principal. If clients don't want the comprehensive benefits of the full Protective Circle, that's their choice. But they must at least understand what they're choosing to include and not include in the protective programs they ultimately select and rely on.

Second, protection providers can use the Protective Circle as a rough template for designing and planning comprehensive protection programs. This encourages us to consider the interconnectedness between protective tasks, organization, capabilities, training, and more. Even though some programs are bigger and more complex than others, at some level, every agent and every team lead needs to think through every aspect of the Protective Circle every day.

Third, both providers and client organizations alike can use the Protective Circle as a powerful diagnostic tool to evaluate or troubleshoot existing programs. By asking the right questions about each element in the Protective Circle, we can quickly pinpoint what's working and what isn't and gain a better understanding of overall program health.

Before we get to all of these things, however, let's take a closer look at each part of the Protective Circle in turn.

Security Needs

WHO we protect and WHY

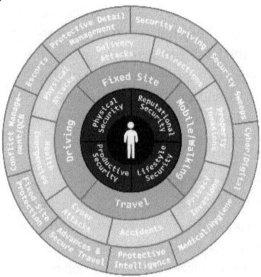

At the center of the Protective Circle are our principals, the **WHO** of executive protection, and **WHY** they need our services: the four fundamental security needs that all executive protection principals have in common.

In fact, all humans share these needs to some extent, but most people are not in the position to hire service providers to help them meet those needs. While some of these needs might not appear to relate to security at first glance, we will make the case that they all directly influence the protective well-being of our principals.

Physical security

Simply put, this is survival, the most basic of all security needs. Our principals need to stay out of harm's way, so they require protection that keeps them alive and healthy as they pursue their professional and other interests.

Productive security

Our principals need to use their time and attention in whatever way creates the most value for themselves and their interests. Because they need to maximize their productivity — and because the business case for paying others to help them do this is clear — they need protection that allows them to increase their focus on things with a higher value add and decrease their focus on more "fundamental" goals such as staying alive as they move from A to B.

Reputational security

The personal brands of our principals are often intertwined with the enterprises they lead. Whether or not what happens to the principal affects share prices and brand equity (and they often do), our principals require protection of their own and their companies' public perception. At the very least, such protection must not negatively affect their reputation.

Lifestyle security

While they might be prominent corporate leaders, our principals are also people. They might be parents interested in giving their children as "normal" an upbringing as possible. Perhaps they like to go for a run in the morning. And chances are they live in relationships that have their ups and downs. Like the rest of us, they'll have their pet peeves, passions, and beliefs about what makes life good or bad. Our principals require protection that supports the lifestyle they choose, not protection that dictates their lifestyle.

Why we need security

We think it's useful to compare these four personal security needs to Maslow's well-known hierarchy of needs[2]. Although the match is not one-to-one, there are many overlaps.

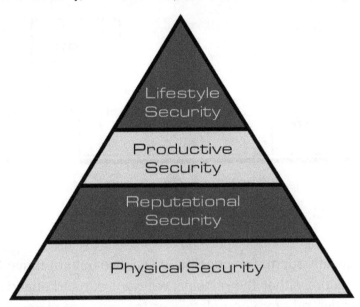

Unsurprisingly, the most fundamental of our four personal security needs, physical security, maps easily onto Maslow's two lowest tiers, the physiological and safety needs that are essential to survival.

What's surprising is that most people, including many in client organizations and far too many who work in the industry as protection providers, equate physical security with the entirety of executive protection and forget about the rest of Maslow's pyramid and three of the four personal security needs outlined above.

To be sure, physical security is the sine qua non — absolutely essential thing — of executive protection and will always be prioritized. Without physical security, there's no executive protection. Although necessary, it's far from sufficient.

Within the context of executive protection, all four personal security needs must be understood as interrelated. The need for physical security is the most obvious, of course: Unless the principal survives, the other three don't matter. However, in the long run, unless the other three security needs are met satisfactorily, marginal increases in physical security won't justify the restrictions they might impose on the principal's

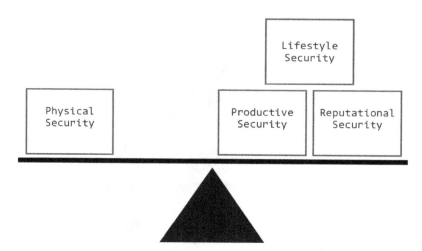

personal freedom. The principal will survive but not thrive. When this occurs, either the principal will want out and abandon the protective program completely, or the program elements that focus on physical security will become so watered down that they won't mitigate risk sufficiently. Either way, the result is the same, and the principal ends up not getting the protection that their risk profile would otherwise recommend.

It's the need for physical security that almost always incentivizes a new protection program. What usually ends them, however, is how well the program also meets the needs for productive, lifestyle, and reputational security.

Now that I've covered the **why** of a comprehensive approach to personal security, it's time to look at the **where** and **when**.

Security Contexts

WHERE and WHEN principals need protection

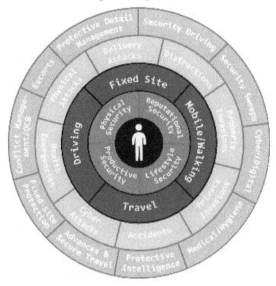

Practically all executive protection takes place in just four security contexts. Seen from the principal's point of view, these contexts merely refer to the various ways and places they spend time. Seen from the protector's perspective, however, each of these four contexts is associated with a different mix of vulnerabilities. The probability of any given threat may vary accordingly. Comprehensive protection programs are designed to mitigate risk equally well in all four contexts, although the nature of risk mitigation often differs according to context.

Fixed sites

Fixed sites are the places where our principals spend solid chunks of time in one spot, regularly or irregularly. These include homes and secondary residences, offices and corporate campuses, hotels, and other temporary lodgings, etc. This category also includes places at which principals spend less time, such as stadiums, theaters, or greenrooms at convention centers.

Even for the most nomadic principals, fixed-site security matters simply because it represents such a significant proportion of each day's 24 hours. If there's no or poor security here, then the Protective Circle is far from complete. Time and place predictability add additional urgency: Compared to when the principal is traveling, it's relatively easier for the bad guys to figure out where and when the principal will be in fixed sites and plan accordingly.

Tactically, fixed-site or "static" security is different from other types of security. Fixed sites may include perimeters, shells, and cells that each provide some level of protection that executive protection professionals work with — and each has their own vulnerabilities. For example, corporate campuses might be surrounded by fences and patrolled by guards, and office buildings typically feature some kind of access control. All of these contribute to the principal's personal protection but don't necessarily guarantee it. Walls can be climbed, doors can be breached, and windows can be broken. Similarly, the mix of protective agents and their capabilities, procedures, and technology will be different for fixed sites compared to other security contexts.

There's sometimes a tendency in the executive protection industry to rank fixed site security as less important than other sections of the Protective Circle such as mobile and walking security or advances and secure travel. In this view, residential security is for lower-paid guards, while accompanying the boss on a trip to Nigeria is for rock-star agents. We think that's wrong. Why would protecting principals where they spend most of their time be less important than protecting them where they travel only occasionally?

As we learned during the COVID-19 pandemic, fixed-site security became even more important when principals spent more time working from home and deliveries of online purchases grew exponentially. In addition to a greater focus on mail and package scanning, the growth of remote working led to many other changes as protective teams adapted to significant lifestyle changes.

Of course, alongside physical security, the principal's other security needs also play a vital role at fixed sites. The integration of the principal's needs for lifestyle autonomy, productivity, and reputational security in the design and implementation of protective programs at fixed sites is essential to sustainable program success.

Mobile/walking

This is the stuff that people outside the industry most often associate with executive protection. The principal is walking from A to B, and "security agents," often muscular men dressed in black suits, get between the boss and the crowd. Even executive protection schools spend an inordinate share of class time nerding around the relative utility of the wedge, box, diamond, and one-to-one formations.

This isn't to say that mobile and walking security isn't important. It is. Although this is not where principals spend most of their time, this is when plenty of things can and do go wrong. The range of vulnerabilities that principals are exposed to walking down a busy street is much larger than what they face sitting in an office or at home. Pies and paint get thrown, paparazzi get punched, and bodyguards get their 15 seconds of fame, or, more precisely, infamy. And the principal gets embarrassed or worse.

Mobile/walking security is another great place to remember the interrelatedness of the four security needs discussed above. Yes, physical security is vital when the principal is on the move, but it must be balanced with the principal's other security needs, not least reputational and lifestyle security. That's why thinking outside of the box formation is so important, and one reason that "covert" protection (another word for "professional" protection?) is gaining in popularity. Often, it's more important that agents blend in rather than stick out. Whether they're walking, running, pushing a baby buggy, or riding a bicycle, few corporate principals are interested in looking like they need the Secret Service to get from a car into a building.

Driving

Whether commuting to work, getting around town, or traveling, our principals spend a lot of time in vehicles. Making this time as safe and productive as possible is a central task for executive protection professionals.

Vulnerability to traffic accidents is clearly an issue when the principal is within meters of other drivers propelling tons of metal at speed. But vulnerability to kidnapping is also much greater on the road than in fixed sites.

Again, some in this industry view security driving as somehow less important than other aspects of executive protection. Again, I beg to differ. For one thing, no matter what country you're in, road accidents are much more probable than terrorist and other attacks and rank high on any list of predictable and mitigatable risks. For another, although it might look easy to the untrained eye, security drivers must master a variety of skills that far surpass those of the average motorist.

In addition to learning advanced defensive and evasive tactics, security drivers must have a solid understanding of basic vehicle dynamics, be able to find the best routes, and adjust controls without taking their eyes off the road. The drivers that excel also have the customer service skills of a consummate concierge and protect the principal's productivity with the vehemence of the most dedicated agent.

Providing this service for principals in their hometowns is one thing. Ensuring the same quality of service whether the principal is in Kathmandu or Kansas is quite another, which leads us to our next stop on the Protective Circle.

Travel

As most principals spend a good share of their time away from home, secure travel is another vital component of comprehensive protection. While it's true that time spent traveling will typically be either in fixed sites, driving, walking, or flying, we want to treat the travel context separately because the unpredictability of new and unknown places means we can't always ensure the same levels of physical, productive, reputational, and lifestyle security on the road as we can at home.

Advances are what reduce this unpredictability and the other frictions of travel to a manageable level.

In a nutshell, executive protection advances are the preparation and planning for a trip to a specific place at a specific time. Whether the trip is for a few hours to the other side of town or a multi-country junket that lasts weeks, the principles are the same. After a briefing on the agenda and goals for the trip — informed by a solid understanding of the principal's productivity and lifestyle preferences — one or more agents will go to the destination to assess the various venues included in the itinerary and determine the best routes between them. Identifying location-specific threats, such as POIs known or suspected to be in an area, could be one part of an advance. Assessing location-specific vulnerabilities is another. Good advances enable good project management of efficient trips that live up to agreed standards.

Among the many problems advances can prevent are those that stem from using third-party vendors when far from home. Unlike US presidents whose limos and security drivers are flown in wherever the president goes, executive protection teams are responsible for sourcing and vetting cars and drivers all around the world. They might also need to contract local pilots, technical surveillance counter measures (TSCM) specialists, chefs, and medics. Good advances increase the probability of everything clicking according to plan and reduce the likelihood of preventable travel SNAFUs.

The more time there is to prepare for a trip, the better. But the principal's schedule can change abruptly for any number of reasons. That's why good protection agents and teams find ways to create the best advances time and budgets allow and are able to improvise on the run.

Threats and Vulnerabilities
WHAT principals need protection against

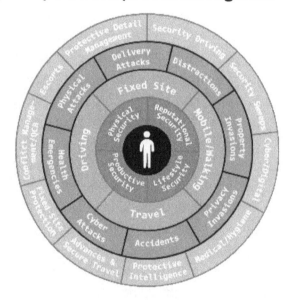

With our definition of risk in mind, let's now consider the nine categories of threats and vulnerabilities. Each threat will have its own range of vulnerabilities to them. For example, the threat of a physical attack will have different vulnerabilities depending on when the principal is where (e.g., walking, driving, traveling, or in a fixed site) and might thus require different risk mitigation procedures. As we'll see, the threats and vulnerabilities we're concerned with here are personal, i.e., they can lead to the harm of an individual principal's physical, reputational, productive, or lifestyle security. Of course, these threats and vulnerabilities might also elevate risk for other people, too.

Our list of threats and vulnerabilities is intentionally short. We choose not to go into any detail on the many possible variations that each of these categories could include — that would be beyond the scope of *The Protective Circle*. Nonetheless, for the purpose of introducing the importance of comprehensive executive protection, I believe this overview suffices.

Threats and Vulnerabilities

Physical Attacks

Examples	Bodily harm from people, weapons, explosives, and other devices; physical harassment (e.g., getting "pied" or splashed with paint); kidnappings. Persons and groups of interest (POIs and GOIs) and persons to be on the lookout for (BOLOs).
Why they matter	Physical attacks — on themselves and their loved ones — are probably the primary reason most principals seek protection. While their probability compared to other risks is relatively low, their impact can be severe in the extreme.

Property Invasions

Examples	Home and workplace invasions; burglaries; trespassing
Why they matter	Unwanted incursions violate principals' private spaces. While theft of private property is always an associated risk, things can be replaced. The bigger associated risks are physical attacks and privacy invasions.

Privacy Invasions

Examples	Paparazzi; stalkers; gawkers; unwanted public interactions

Why they matter	Privacy invasions — whether they occur while the principal is at home or out in the world — are particularly troublesome for prominent people. While recognizability comes with the territory of prominence and celebrity, principals must be able to decide when to interact with others who "want a piece of them."

Accidents

Examples	Traffic accidents; accidents while working/traveling/relaxing
Why they matter	Although physical attacks and property invasions get much more attention than accidents, it's road accidents that are the most probable — and their consequences can be just as devastating.

Natural Disasters

Examples	Earthquakes, storms, wildfires
Why they matter	Although rare and completely impersonal, natural disasters pose a real threat to everyone — especially in certain places. Comprehensive protection programs should always consider the likelihood and possible impact of these events.

Health Emergencies

Examples	Sudden medical conditions that require immediate first aid, e.g., heart attacks, cuts, falls; risks related to allergies, viruses, poor hygienic conditions, etc.
Why they matter	If untreated, health emergencies can be anything from bothersome to lethal. Quick intervention from trained protection agents doesn't replace professional health care, but it can in some cases be sufficient and in others be a lifesaving bridge to the emergency room.

Cyberattacks	
Examples	Personal cyber/digital attacks such as hacked personal devices, technical surveillance and bugs, exposure to insecure Wi-Fi, etc.
Why they matter	Corporate principals who benefit from vigilant IT departments with deep expertise in cybersecurity are often on the road, where cyber-protection is far less structured and threats are more likely.

Delivery Attacks	
Examples	Mail and parcel attacks; powders and explosive devices; risks related to takeaway food deliveries
Why they matter	Like the rest of us, principals and their families/organizations are making more online purchases than ever. While personal access to principals is often limited by security procedures, in many cases these same principals are relatively easy to reach directly with mail, parcel, and food deliveries.

Distractions	
Examples	Time and attention spent dealing with the frictions of daily commutes, travel, and unwanted interactions
Why they matter	Distractions are a risk to productive security, not to physical security. While they aren't lethal or expensive per se, they do cost what many otherwise wealthy people have in short supply: time and attention. Situations that remove the principal's focus from their most productive self, including the distraction of their own security team, are thus a risk in their own right. The mitigation of this risk can be a very tangible benefit of protection programs primarily designed to mitigate other risk types.

Protective Capabilities
HOW principals receive protection

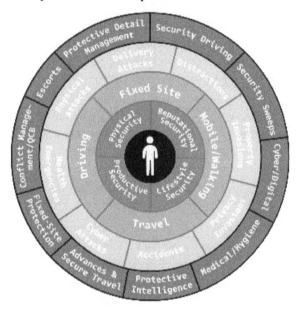

Mitigation of the risks that may emerge from the threats and vulnerabilities outlined above is the meat and bones of executive protection. Accordingly, the protective team must master a range of competencies to prevent these risks from reaching principals in the first place — and deal with them directly if prevention fails.

See **Section 3: The Importance of Training** to dig into the training needs of executive protection agents and teams. Here, see a brief overview of the capabilities that form the outer ring of the Protective Circle and why they matter. Some of these skill sets relate directly to one of the four security contexts outlined above — others are useful in multiple or all contexts.

Protective Capabilities

Conflict Management/Close-Quarters Battle

Examples	Conflict de-escalation; tactical defense, close-quarters battle (CQB), unarmed combat; armed combat
Why they matter	Preventing physical attacks on the principal is the first (and usually only) competence most people associate with executive protection. Although this skill set unfortunately gets more attention than most others, it's indeed essential: in case of hostile aggressors, agents must be able to deflect attacks and get the principal to safety. This category of competency will always include conflict de-escalation and unarmed combat skills. Depending on the nature of the program, it may also include armed interventions. In all cases, knowing when to use which form of conflict management is absolutely essential.

Security Driving

Examples	Defensive and evasive driving; customer service; navigation
Why they matter	Principals spend a lot of time in vehicles while commuting and traveling. On almost any given day, unintentional traffic accidents are among the highest-probability risks. What's more, planned attacks often take place on the road where time and place predictability can give perpetrators tactical advantages. Good security driving does more than prevent accidents and kidnapping. It also enables the principal to use driving time as productively as possible.

Medical/Hygiene	
Examples	First aid and emergency medical skills; hygiene procedures that reduce the likelihood of contagion and infections
Why they matter	Executive protection agents aren't doctors, but they might be called on to provide first aid in case of medical health emergencies. Knowing how to provide CPR, stop bleeding, or use an EpiPen can have life-and-death importance anywhere. In developing countries where ambulance response times can be much longer than seven minutes, they can be even more critical.
Cyber/Digital	
Examples	Operating alarms and sensors; ensuring secure connections
Why they matter	In our increasingly connected world, technology plays an important role in many aspects of executive protection: threats, vulnerabilities, and risk mitigation. Agents must be tech-savvy enough to know how technology can be used as a threat and how technology can open and close vulnerability to threats. Importantly, agents must also have a good sense of their own technical competencies (or lack thereof) and when to ask dedicated experts for more help.
Protective Intelligence	
Examples	Risk, threat, and vulnerability assessments (RTVAs); travel intelligence; surveillance detection; social listening; POIs, GOIs, BOLOs

Why they matter	Risk mitigation starts with a clear understanding of the actual and potential threats and vulnerabilities facing a principal. Protective intelligence is how agents improve their understanding of these risks. The priority here is on actionable intelligence that's pertinent to the well-being of the principal. Unlike corporate intelligence departments which are also concerned with things like supply chains and political stability, an agent's focus is on personal risk in the near term, not corporate risk in the long term.
Advances and Secure Travel	
Examples	Advances; travel logistics; concierge/ customer service
Why they matter	Executive protection principals often have heavy travel schedules. Making trips as safe, productive, and friction-free as possible requires a range of competencies. Knowing how to do the pre-trip advances that are crucial to smooth execution is essential, but even careful plans can get changed at a moment's notice. Protective teams must ensure reliable logistics for people and their baggage, moving principals and their entourages through airports, hotels, office and conference complexes, African savannas, and wherever else the principal's business or personal interests take them.
Protective Detail Management	
Examples	Team management; vendor management; financial planning and reporting; managing the relationship between the protective team and the team at the principal's organization
Why they matter	Whether they're part of an internal security department or belong to an outside vendor, in addition to running protection, executive protection managers also run a business.

Why they matter (cont'd)	Among many other things, managers must ensure that agreed procedures, standards, and budgets are met, communication with principals and their stakeholders are smooth, and expense reports are accurate and get sent on time.

Security Sweeps

Examples	Mail and parcel screening; IEDs, technical surveillance counter measures (TSCM); canine
Why they matter	In addition to physical protection against delivery attacks and IED plants, bugging and other forms of electronic eavesdropping are an unfortunate reality that rarely gets much publicity but does real harm.

Security Escorts

Examples	Mobile formations, covert protection
Why they matter	Getting the principal safely from one secured location to another is a critical part of any protection program. Doing it discreetly (aka "covert protection") and without looking like the Secret Service is a priority for many contemporary principals. Poorly done security escorts are when many of the unfortunate incidents between "bodyguards" and paparazzi take place and make the news.

Fixed-Site Protection

Examples	Protecting perimeters, shells, and cells; manning and running security operation centers; setting up and using alarm, CCTV, and sensor systems
Why they matter	Principals spend a lot of time in fixed sites. Working with or without other security stakeholders, protective agents must master a range of skills to make protection as effective and efficient as possible.

A map isn't the territory – but it's still helpful

The Protective Circle is a model that helps explain why executive protection programs exist, what agents do, and the skills they need to function effectively. Those who want to reorganize or pick and choose categories are welcome to adapt the Protective Circle to their needs. As long as the comprehensive nature of solid protective programs is respected, that's fine with me.

Key Takeaways	
The Protective Circle is a model for understanding and planning comprehensive executive protection	
1	**The Center — the WHO and WHY of executive protection** The innermost ring represents the people we protect and the four fundamental security needs that all executive protection principals have in common: • Physical security • Productive security • Reputational security • Lifestyle security
2	**Ring 1 — The WHERE and WHEN of executive protection** The first ring represents the four security contexts in which principals spend most of their time: • Fixed sites • Mobile/walking • Driving • Travel

Key Takeaways	
3	**Ring 2 — WHAT executive protection protects against** This ring comprises the nine categories of threats and vulnerabilities that are the primary concern of executive protection: • Physical attacks • Property invasions • Privacy invasions • Accidents • Natural disasters • Health emergencies • Cyberattacks • Delivery attacks • Distractions
4	**Ring 3 — the HOW of executive protection** The outermost ring indicates the 10 protective capabilities that executive protection agents and teams must master to provide suitable protection: • Conflict management/close-quarters battle (CQB) • Security driving • Medical/hygiene • Cyber/digital • Protective intelligence • Advances and secure travel • Protective detail management • Security sweeps • Security escorts • Fixed-site protection

Chapter 1-3:

Why every corporation and ultra-high-net-worth family should have an executive protection strategy

I'm often asked why corporations and family offices establish executive protection programs for their CEOs and other employees. The question is fair enough since executive protection is a relatively new phenomenon for many organizations, and by its very nature, not something that people outside the boardroom, C-suite, or the industry discuss much in public.

But the more I think about an answer, the more I'm convinced that the question should be turned on its head. A better question is, "Why wouldn't corporations establish executive protection programs for their CEOs and other C-level employees? And what makes ultra-high-net-worth individuals think they face no greater risk than anyone else?"

First, let's try to understand why more and more corporations and family offices are setting up executive protection programs — and why many organizations really should at least consider these six reasons to write a proactive executive protection strategy.

You Already Have an Executive Protection Strategy: Make It Proactive Rather Than Reactive

It's interesting to note that while few large organizations would admit to not having a communication or HR strategy, many of these same organizations have never thought about formulating an executive protection strategy.

Whether it's implicit or explicit, however, every corporation and family office already has an executive protection strategy. The difference is that some organizations base their strategies on a proactive process of risk analysis and mitigation, as outlined above, while others take a more laissez-faire and reactive approach, employing a wait-and-see strategy that only changes when circumstances demand it.

A corporate protection program should ideally be for all employees. After all, duty of care applies to everyone in the corporation, high and low, and the risks of doing one's job can apply at many levels. For example, a service technician traveling to a Boko Haram-controlled area of Nigeria is clearly exposed to tangible threats. So is a highly prominent CEO speaking at a public event in New York.

As we'll see below, however, there are a number of reasons why more comprehensive versions of this service are usually reserved for members of the C-suite.

Executive Protection Safeguards Shareholder Investment in C-Level Personnel

For some CEO positions, board-mandated executive protection programs come with the territory. Or should.

The CEO's prominence is one factor that plays into this, as highly prominent business leaders are more at risk from "persons of interest" precisely due to their notoriety. Some CEOs are often in the news nationally and internationally for one reason or another. They might work in an industry that's in the public spotlight or is controversial, or their personal success and details of their wealth might be the subject of financial and gossip magazines.

As public figures, many people recognize CEOs and ultra-high-net-worth individuals and are fascinated by them, by how they live, and even by their families. Persons of interest might have a grudge, they might be in love, or they might be looking for a handout since their own income is considerably lower than the CEO's. They could also be potential kidnappers. In any case, risk analyses often show that the potential threats to a highly prominent CEO can be equal to or greater than those of other "celebrities" with whom they would never otherwise compare themselves.

But boards also consider the business and investor impact of an accident occurring to the CEO. As has been amply demonstrated by a number of unfortunate incidents, corporate reputations and share prices can be closely linked to an individual CEO's well-being.

When shareholder value can rise or fall dramatically with the safety of a CEO, it's natural that boards choose to safeguard their investment in the CEO with protection programs that cost a fraction of their overall compensation package.

Executive Protection Enables Higher Productivity of the Highest Paid

There's a reason CEOs have personal assistants, travel by company jet or in business class, and don't have to write up the minutes of every meeting they participate in — productivity. The CEO is usually the highest-paid person not just in the room, but in the company.

Executive protection, in addition to keeping people safe, also enables higher productivity by making travel and everyday logistics as smooth as possible.

Secure travel eliminates waiting for cabs and standing at the car rental counter. Unlike a ride with a chatty (and often unvetted and potentially dangerous) limo driver, it minimizes interruptions, turns travel time into work time, and lets high-paid execs pack more meetings in more places into less time than most other people can even fathom.

Executive Protection Enables More Frequent, Safer Travel

One of my clients once said something that has stuck with me ever since: "You guys make it easier to travel, so we travel more."

It's really as simple as that.

The CEO is typically the corporation's best salesman, evangelist, and negotiator all rolled into one. Executive protection takes a lot of the friction and hassle out of traveling. So, the CEO gets more face time with customers, employees, government officials, and other key stakeholders worldwide.

Duty of Care

"Duty of care" is a term usually heard in one of two places: courts of law trying negligence cases and marketing blurbs from executive protection companies fishing for business.

Plenty has been written about "duty of care" elsewhere, so I'll keep my take on this short. Yes, companies and individuals can be and are held liable for failing to adhere to reasonable levels of care in order to prevent injury. No, mentioning "duty of care" doesn't mean the head of every company (or anyone else employed by the company) should be getting an extensive personal protection program.

According to law.com, duty of care is:

> "a requirement that a person act toward others and the public with the watchfulness, attention, caution and prudence that a reasonable person in the circumstances would use. If a person's actions do not meet this standard of care, then the acts are considered negligent, and any damages resulting may be claimed in a lawsuit for negligence."

To paraphrase concerning corporate executive protection:

> "Given the circumstances (prominence, threat levels, risk analyses, etc.) of their CEOs and other employees, many boards, after benchmarking with similar organizations, find it prudent and reasonable to meet a certain standard of care (including executive protection) in order to reduce liability and for the other five reasons presented here."

Executive Protection Can Provide a Competitive Advantage

Everything else being equal, if one corporation's C-level executives are more productive and safer than another's, that's a competitive boost. What board wouldn't want its CEO to be safer and more productive? And maybe even more motivated because they can enjoy the benefits of a well-conceived executive protection strategy.

	Key Takeaways
	Family offices and corporations have six good reasons to create executive protection strategies
1	**You already have an executive protection strategy: Make it proactive** Organizations which haven't articulated an explicit strategy for protecting their principals (and other people) still have a strategy, but "do nothing until we are forced to" is not the most effective one.
2	**Executive protection safeguards shareholder investment in C-level personnel** In addition to the personal consequences of something happening to a principal, the effects on a company's market value can also be significant. The monetary and other costs of a protection program should in some cases be seen as an insurance premium, not a perk.
3	**Executive protection enables higher productivity of the highest paid** The productivity benefits of executive protection are often underlooked. However, they can be quite substantial and should be considered when deciding whether and how to set up a program.
4	**Executive protection enables more frequent, safer travel** Since executive protection programs make it easier to travel — with less friction and more productivity — principals often travel more, which can benefit their organizations.

Key Takeaways	
5	**Duty of care** Organizations can face legal consequences for neglecting to care properly for their employees.
6	**Executive protection can provide a competitive advantage** Enhancing the productivity and satisfaction of key employees by providing executive protection can give corporations a competitive edge.

Chapter 1-4:

The questions boards of directors must ask before mandating an executive protection program

Family offices and corporations make decisions regarding the nature and scope of executive protection in different ways. Individuals and families, often via family offices, typically make such decisions on their own and sometimes use consultants for advice. Corporations, especially those that are publicly traded, often involve board-level approval.

However, when it comes to corporate executive protection, no two companies are alike. Every corporation has different needs, cultures, locations, and last but not least, principals with their own requirements and preferences.

But while there's nothing "one size fits all" about corporate executive protection implementation, the questions a board asks before mandating a corporate executive protection program should be basically the same every time. I say "should be" because they often aren't. Too many companies jump, slide, or limp into an executive protection program without first considering all their options. Instead, they should use the Protective Circle to ask at least three questions.

Who Will Be Protected, from What – and What Are Our Options?

Few corporate or family office boards have expertise in executive protection. Unlike other issues on the agenda at board meetings, the distinctions between sub-standard, common, and best practice regarding executive protection programs may seem unclear and unproven to board members. Whereas few boards would doubt what distinguishes unacceptable from great financial reporting, for example, even fewer are likely to have an informed opinion about the elements of a best-in-class executive protection solution — let alone a minimally viable executive protection program.

Given this lack of expertise in an area that might impact the corporation's key principals or even its market value, it's no wonder that many boards have a difficult time deciding whether or not to mandate a corporate executive protection program. That's why they often ask for benchmarking with similar organizations. What are their principals' risk profiles? How do their protective programs mitigate personal security risks? What's involved? How much does it cost?

All protective programs should ideally start with our equivalent of the situation analysis: an RTVA. RTVAs describe the principal's personal security situation, usually with particular focus on the threats and vulnerabilities that comprise risk, and lay the foundation for subsequent risk mitigation.

Depending on circumstances, RTVAs might also be prepared for spouses or children as well as additional corporate principals.

Where and When Will They Be Protected?

Some executive protection programs begin on an ad hoc basis, e.g., with travel to high-risk areas. Some are only for work-related travels and activities. Still, others are designed for true 24/7/365 coverage, no matter where the principal's work or other interests take them.

Whether your executive protection program is designed to provide comprehensive, round-the-clock protection or more limited security should depend on the outcome of the RTVA and the resultant program objectives. Minimally viable programs typically start with the highest-risk circumstances.

Just where the employee should be protected is a key question that every executive protection strategy must answer. As principals move through their work and personal lives, they travel through a wide variety of locations, each with its particular advantages and disadvantages from a security point of view.

Best-in-class executive protection programs must be ready to function wherever the principals' lifestyles take them. Minimally viable programs will focus on those locations that represent the highest risks, and mitigate those. Whether or not — and to what extent — the program will include all conceivable locations should depend on the risk analysis and executive protection strategy.

Places to consider include:

- At the principal's residence
- During commutes to and from work
- At work
- While traveling
- At public or semi-public events
- At other family members' activities

At the principal's residence

The principal's residence should be covered by both an alarm and a video system that are monitored 24/7/365 at a dedicated central station either on the property or remotely.

In addition to this electronic surveillance, protection agents can be deployed in a number of ways.

Some of these options, listed below in order of increasing effectiveness, are:

Option 1	Contract with a third-party security provider to monitor residential alarm and video systems and respond if needed.
Option 2	One or several security agents provide coverage from vehicles parked outside the property. With access to alarms and video feeds, they provide a deterrent and can respond to privacy or security threats. The agents are connected to a remote security operations center (SOC) for communication, reporting, and support.
Option 3	Two agents provide coverage from within the property. Working in shifts 24/7/365, one agent monitors alarms and video feeds, and the other provides a response. The SOC is a room on the property with its own facilities for the security agents, so coverage is continuous despite restroom or meal breaks.
Option 4	Add protective surveillance and anti-surveillance teams to Option 3 in order to monitor movements outside the property.

During commutes to and from work

The predictability of the times and locations involved with commuting between home and work increases the risk of attack or harassment. There are a number of options regarding how to protect principals during their daily commutes. Some of these are listed below, but the one that is right for your program will depend on the outcome of a reliable executive protection contractor's analysis and recommendations.

Among other criteria, choosing the best option relies on an understanding of risk and risk tolerance and on the principal's personal preferences.

Option 1	Provide a vehicle with a trained security driver to the principal for their commute to and from work. The driver should be trained in surveillance detection, evasive/defensive driving, vehicle dynamics, and executive protection. The driver should also have the driving skills of a chauffeur to provide a high level of comfort and service to the employee. An added benefit of this option is, of course, that the principal can stay productive during the commute instead of driving.
Option 2	If the principal prefers to drive themselves, provide a surveillance vehicle for each transfer. This requires a dedicated, discreet security vehicle and two highly trained security agents, so one can effec-tively drive the vehicle while the second is alert to the environments around the principal's vehicle during transit. It also provides a more effective response resource to handle issues and threats to the employee.

At work

One or more executive protection agents can be assigned to stay in the vicinity of the principal while at work. These executive protection agents are tasked with immediate response in case of any issues or threats. An additional executive protection agent should cover the corporate SOC to monitor alarms and video feeds.

While traveling

An effective travel protection program includes advance work, redundancy of resources, and of course, proper talent selection. Best-practice travel protection support typically includes:

- Two executive protection agents — one for advances and one for close-in protection. The two EPAs should travel to the destination(s) in advance of the principal's arrival with enough time to prepare both security and logistics plans using industry best practices and advance-work techniques. They must also ensure the quality and appropriateness of all drivers and vehicles. For higher-risk or more complex destinations, vetted and reliable contracted executive protection resources should be utilized at the destination(s) for additional team support.

- A primary vehicle and security-trained driver for transporting the principal and others in their party.

- A backup vehicle and security-trained driver to be used for additional group members and as a quick replacement for the primary vehicle in case the primary becomes unavailable for any reason (mechanical issues, road traffic accident, etc.).

- An advance vehicle and security-trained driver that's used by the advance agent to move ahead of the employee (30–60 minutes) to ensure the next destination is safe and properly prepared for an efficient and appropriate arrival.

Two of the many considerations applicable here are whether such protection should be provided whenever the principal is outside their home or office, or only for work-related travel.

At public or semi-public events

If the principal is required to participate in corporate or other events that are open to the public — say, an annual shareholders' meeting — then it's important that the security around such participation is adequate.

While close personal protection of the principal would be an expected part of the executive protection program, dedicated event security procedures might also be relevant both to safeguard all employees and shareholders and to protect the corporation's overall interests from threats.

At other family members' activities

If the executive protection program includes other family members in addition to the principal, then those individuals will also require close personal protection wherever their schedules and lifestyles take them.

This can include school and extracurricular activities for children, work and leisure activities for spouses, etc.

What Kinds of Protective Capabilities Are Necessary?

Truly comprehensive executive protection programs deploy the Protective Circle's 10 protective capabilities, in varying degrees, across the four security contexts (fixed sites, driving, travel, mobile/walking) described in **Chapter 1-2**. But many programs begin with much less.

Minimally viable executive protection programs typically include some combination of four elements:

1. Alarm monitoring, access control, and trained security agents for controlling access to the principal's workplace and residence
2. Security drivers trained in executive protection and defensive/evasive driving

3. Automobile(s) specially equipped
   for security
4. Flights on corporate/private aircraft
   for business and personal purposes

This combination of access control and secure transportation can be considered the "baby steps" of corporate executive protection, and this is the right way to begin.

Best-practice executive protection programs include two more basic elements:

5. Close personal protection provided by
   trained and carefully selected executive
   protection agents at all times, or
   most of the time, whether the principal
   is at home, at work, moving around in
   public, while traveling, or even while
   on holiday
6. Protective intelligence resources
   that monitor, investigate, and report
   on people of interest, inappropriate
   communications, and threats, and also
   provide risk analysis and travel
   risk assessments for the principal's
   scheduled trips and events

The most extensive programs often add two more elements that simultaneously increase security and minimize its visibility:

7. Surveillance and anti-surveillance
   protection that identifies and deters
   potential attackers prior to any attack
8. Covert protection that utilizes
   specially trained agents who provide
   security but keep their distance

A Good Executive Protection Program Is More Than the Sum of Its Parts

Now that we've lined up the elements of a good executive protection program, let's be clear about one more thing: A corporate executive protection program is about much more than choosing from a catalog of elements.

In our experience, the success of corporate executive protection also depends on:

- An effective understanding of how the executive protection program integrates with the rest of the corporate organization
- Knowledge of and respect for the principal's lifestyle and personal preferences as regards executive protection
- An intelligent and thorough executive protection strategy
- Well-trained and carefully selected executive protection staff

Key Takeaways	
1	Before boards of directors mandate executive protection programs, they need to ask a range of questions and consider a range of options regarding the scope and scale of the risk mitigation. Broadly speaking, these considerations include: • Who will be protected? • When will they be protected? • What kinds of protection are necessary? • Where should they be protected?
2	Similarly, boards should have at least a rudimentary understanding of the differences between "good enough," common, and best-practice corporate executive protection.

Chapter 1-5:

Some of the most common questions we get from new executive protection clients concern staffing levels. What are our options? What have principals with similar needs done before us? How many people do we need to set up a program, and what kinds of people do they need to be?

This is a natural line of questioning. Those tasked with starting up new protection programs often have little or no experience in the field or track record for reference. This can also be the case for those with protective backgrounds from the government: cultural norms can be completely different between the public and private sectors, as can budgetary considerations and organizational expectations.

This is a crucial line of questioning with a lot riding on the answers. Program success depends directly on the quality and quantity of staffing levels. Programs that are understaffed lead to burn-out, invite favoritism, and generally perform poorly, defeating our purpose of keeping the principal safe and productive. Ultimately, they fail to demonstrate their value, and will either be replaced or terminated — often along with those responsible for making the staffing decisions.

In addition to their performance and operational issues, under-developed protection programs usually suffer a slow death for other reasons. When those tasked with managing and organizing the program get stuck in the tactical weeds of doing endless shifts, they neglect their strategic leadership roles. They simply don't have, and should not be expected to have, the bandwidth to be both the on-the-ground protective agents and to establish and maintain the necessary relationships throughout the corporate or family office ecosystems. Thus, there is no one to create and maintain transparency between the program and other stakeholders or work for a shared understanding of program value — the consequences of which can be as debilitating for sustainable program viability as poor operational performance.

So How Do You Staff a Good Executive Protection Program?

As we have pointed out many times before, there are no cookie-cutter protection solutions. Staffing levels for executive protection depend on program goals, which in turn must be needs-based. And the only real way to determine a principal's risk mitigation needs is to perform an RTVA which takes into account the principal's prominence, known threats, work and travel routines, personal preferences, and a host of other factors. Only once this improved situational awareness has been established should staffing be considered.

What are the staffing variables?

Those responsible for introducing executive protection services to the corporation must present staffing needs in a way that's understandable to others who most often have no experience in the field. To do this, it's helpful to break things down along the lines of the most important variables that must be considered.

The single most important staffing variable is **coverage**: when and in which situations does the principal require protection, and how much protection is necessary? The explanatory scenarios below show that coverage needs to vary from occasional (for example, only when traveling to relatively high-risk locations) to 24/7/365. It's important to remember here both the principal's personal preferences and any organizational culture issues, and that what a principal may want in terms of coverage (for example, as little and as unobtrusive as possible) may not be what a board-mandated program would prescribe (as comprehensive as possible).

In addition to coverage, or time spent protecting the principal, consider the Protective Circle's 10 protective capabilities and the **training** necessary to build or maintain these. Some executive protection skills are rarely used but critical to have; others are perishable and need to be refreshed on a regular basis (see more about this in `Section 3: The Importance of Training`). Training needs must be addressed openly as part of staffing-level discussions.

The other key staffing variable is the **types of personnel** needed. The most common choices here are the protective program manager and protective agents, but other roles such as security drivers, residential agents, intelligence analysts, and more may also be relevant in more comprehensive programs.

Next, consider the **make/buy decision**. Although a needs-based staff headcount should (everything else being equal) remain the same whether or not all or parts of the program are outsourced, organizational relationships do make a difference. For example, hiring a specialist partner with enough bandwidth can allow the corporation to benefit from scale advantages more flexibly without ramping up headcount.

Finally, we also need to understand **the availability of other corporate or family office security resources** upon which the executive protection program can draw. If a corporation already has its own intelligence analysts or global security operations center (GSOC), for example, this can impact the scope of the executive protection program and headcount.

Scenario 1: Staffing a part-time executive protection program

Let's start with the simplest program, one that provides protection only in very limited circumstances, part-time, e.g., when the principal occasionally travels to high-risk countries or has the rare speaking engagement at a high-profile event where controversy is expected. Here, both executive protection agents and security drivers will be needed on an ad hoc basis.

In this case, the question of full-time staffing has a simple answer: Don't bother. It's far more efficient to rely on a specialist partner to meet such executive protection needs as needed rather than contracting full-time employees.

Scenario 2: Staffing a viable full-time executive protection program

I receive the most questions about this scenario in particular. If the corporation needs to protect its CEO while performing their job, what kind of staffing levels should be expected?

To answer this question, we need to make some assumptions. First, let's assume that the CEO has a workweek similar to many of our principals, i.e., an average of 60 hours per week, with spikes up to 80 and slow weeks down to 40.

Then, let's remember that protective agents work even longer hours than the principal. The agent must arrive at the pickup point well before the designated time and leave the final drop-off point only after the principal has been securely installed there and all reporting and prep tasks have been wrapped up, adding an average of two working hours per day to that of the principal. That gives us a weekly total of 10 hours in addition to the principal's 60, or an average of 70 agent hours per week. That's 1.75 full-time agents before we even start talking about training, professional development, paid time off, sick days, etc. So, let's call these two full-time staff.

Let's also assume that the principal travels a week or two out of most months, as most do, both domestically and internationally, often with multiple destinations on each trip. Depending on risk profiles and itineraries this will require at least one additional agent, and typically two if one will be performing advance work while the other is providing close protection and traveling with the principal.

While the traveling duo is on the road, the at-home duo has time to engage in required training or take personal time off, and vice versa.

And let's not forget that the program also needs a manager to organize, develop, provide guidance to, and follow up with the four agents, as well as to interface with other parts of the corporate organization to ensure program success. Placing someone in the double role of manager and working agent isn't a sustainable option; I've never seen it work for long, but have seen it create a lot of problems.

This brings us to a total of four to five full-time staff — one manager and four agents — as a minimally viable executive staff that provides protection during the principal's working hours. This does not include security drivers or other resources, or the nonworking parts of the principal's life. Even with a team of four to five persons, there's still a need for agents to fill in the gaps and be ready for any unexpected rise in demand for services on a global scale.

Scenario 3: Staffing a comprehensive, complex, and multifaceted executive protection program

The last scenario includes everything mentioned above in Scenario 2 and more.

Such complex scenarios typically provide coverage for the rest of the principal's life: residential security for time spent at home, additional executive protection for non-work travel and leisure activities, and protection for spouses and children.

These more comprehensive programs could also comprise protection for multiple corporate principals as well as additional security services including event risk mitigation, intelligence analysis programs, covert protection, surveillance detection, GSOC support, and technical surveillance counter measures (TSCM) and other tech solutions.

There are simply too many to go through all the possible variants of such advanced programs. Suffice it to say that staffing levels increase with additional protectees and services.

Key Takeaways	
1	Program size depends on the principal's security needs as clarified by the RTVA. It also depends on a range of variables: • Coverage needs — when and where principal requires protection — and how much • Agents' professional development needs, e.g., training and physical fitness • Types of protective personnel needed • Whether and to what degree executive protection services are outsourced or insourced • Availability of other security sources available that the executive protection program can use, e.g., intelligence analysts and GSOCs
2	Rough guidelines for appropriate staffing levels (ranging from the simplest to the most complex): • **Scenario 1:** Staffing a part-time executive protection program • **Scenario 2:** Staffing a viable full-time executive protection program • **Scenario 3:** Staffing a comprehensive, complex, and multifaceted executive protection program

Chapter 1-6:

What's the best way for corporations and family offices to source executive protection services?

The "make-or-buy" decision is a classic quandary for manufacturing companies. Is the corporation better off making a product or component on its own, or would it be smarter to buy the product from an external supplier? The same questions arise when companies are faced with the choice of developing and maintaining in-house service capabilities or purchasing these from an external service provider.

Organizations that want to start up, maintain, or turn around executive protection programs must answer their own "make-or-buy" questions. Should they hire their own staff, including executive protection managers, agents, and security drivers? Should they outsource this work to a partner that specializes in executive protection? Or maybe should they aim for a hybrid solution that includes both their own and vendor employees?

Buyer, Beware. Employer, Be Warier.

Decision makers tasked with implementing new executive protection programs face these quandaries with little to guide them. Family offices — whose focus areas include investments, legal matters, philanthropy, taxes, and trusts — will most likely have no relevant experience or even a security director. Corporate security directors without any direct experience with executive protection will also be on their own, and those who turn to colleagues in the procurement department for help may or may not get assistance. Very few procurement managers have any experience in the field, and the personal nature of executive protection for founders, CEOs, and other high-net-worth individuals can be a minefield they are rightfully hesitant to enter. Even budgetary considerations may place such decisions beyond the radar range of corporate procurement departments: There are likely no precedents for dealing with such C-suite costs; the budgets themselves may not be great enough to trigger direct involvement from purchasing watchdogs; and the gray areas between what the company and the individual should pay or be taxed for can be daunting territory for the uninitiated.

Conversely, those responsible for make-or-buy decisions for established, ongoing executive protection programs will most likely have experience dealing with executive protection vendors — whether they also employ some of their own protection staff or not. After all, even the biggest, most complex private-sector programs simply cannot do everything by themselves. Unlike the Secret Service, which flies its own vehicles and drivers to wherever the US president needs to go, no corporate or family office program I've ever heard of maintains its own vehicles and drivers in all the domestic locations its principals travel to — not to mention the international destinations the principal might visit twice a year or once in a lifetime.

So, what makes best sense for corporations and family offices: outsourcing or insourcing executive protection? Well, that depends on many things — beginning with answers to the four questions we ask below, but also including careful consideration of program maturity and complexity, and exactly which parts of the overall program are in play for insourcing or outsourcing.

The Four Key Criteria of Make-or-Buy Analyses

There are dozens of make-or-buy decision models, and no self-respecting consultancy is without its own "unique" take on how to answer this perennial question. A quick glance across many models, however, reveals four basic criteria that practically all decisions are based on — or should be:

1. **Core competence:** Are the competences necessary to deliver the services core to the corporation's strategy and success?
2. **Cost efficiency:** What are the total costs of making or buying the given service — and how do they compare?
3. **Performance capability:** How difficult is it to develop the necessary capabilities? Can an insourced program deliver the same quality and perform as well as best-in-class industry leaders?
4. **Risks:** What are the risks associated with either insourcing or outsourcing the service?

Is executive protection a core competence for your organization?

At the risk of stating the obvious — and unless you're an executive protection company or a governmental organization like the Secret Service — then the answer to this is, "No." I've worked for hundreds of corporations over the years who sell everything from soup to nuts — as well as for dozens of family offices and celebrities — and not one of them was an executive protection company.

However, some corporations and family offices do employ their own executive protection staff, to some extent or another, just as they might for many other "nonessential" services, e.g., cafeterias, cleaning, IT support, and payroll. At the same time, many organizations that depend on abilities so central to their business such as clear strategic thinking and effective communication regularly outsource some of these tasks to consultancies and PR or advertising agencies.

So, why does this question of core competencies even come up? Because it matters — especially regarding questions of human resource management. Executive protection is a people business. The quality of the service depends not least on the quality of the people providing it. Thus, before even considering how agents, processes, and technology must come together to provide good protection, you have to have the people.

Getting HR issues right is neither trivial nor simple. To staff and run an executive protection program without the help of vendors, the organization would need to attract, develop, and retain all of the necessary executive protection talent on its own. That is, the organization would need to become experts in recruiting, interviewing, security screening, training, compensating, onboarding, and off-boarding executive pro-tection managers and agents — just to mention a few HR topics. In my experience, very few do.

The situation is different for specialist executive protection providers. They have a vested interest and experience in finding candidates that have the best chance for long-term success. They appreciate the need for developing people and skills and are accustomed to ensuring that all agents have an annual training program including drills, tabletops, and recurring basic training to keep perishable skills fresh. They can provide advanced training designed to increase agent capabilities and performance quality. They know the importance of spotting talent and encouraging the best to follow career paths of growing expertise and responsibility; and, to retain talent, the bigger providers can provide many more career opportunities than any in-house program. The better-established companies also have helpful networks and good reputations that give them easier access to candidates.

Good specialist partners typically have a deep bench of pre-screened and vetted candidates for executive protection agent and manager positions. If one doesn't work out, for whatever reason, they can be changed quickly and efficiently, usually without the financial and operational consequences of terminating employment.

What's the most cost-efficient way to set up a corporate executive protection program for your company?

Executive protection companies need to make a profit like any other. So, doesn't it make sense for a company or family office to save that profit margin and reduce costs by insourcing? In theory, yes — at least for some positions. In practice, not necessarily. In my experience, rarely for the majority of positions.

When considering the costs of executive protection programs, it's imperative to include all direct and indirect costs, over time, to arrive at a reliable evaluation of total costs of program ownership.

- **Direct costs** are straightforward and relatively simple to define for both insourced and outsourced options. These consist largely of salaries and travel expenses for protective personnel, subcontracting secure-travel communication equipment, vehicles, and vendors (e.g., security drivers, locally based EP agents for domestic and foreign travel).
- **Indirect costs** are also primarily related to program staff, but not as immediately apparent. These include all expenses associated with benefits, bonuses, insurance, recruitment, stock options, terminations, training, turnover, etc.

The Salary Cost Breakdown table summarizes direct and indirect staff costs per executive protection agent at three different salary levels. As the table shows, indirect costs add approximately 40 percent to direct (salary) costs.

In addition to these direct and indirect personnel costs, organizations should also consider the **opportunity costs** of establishing and staffing service functions that are noncore to their business. For example, a software company is presumably an expert in recruiting and developing engineers but has little experience in creating job descriptions for and hiring executive protection specialists. HR and other management time spent on talent for the core business, i.e., hiring new coders, would thus deliver higher ROI than time spent on an unfamiliar, noncore niche such as executive protection.

Recruitment, however, is just one piece of the HR expertise and cost puzzles. Other considerations include staff retention/development and termination. Let's look at both, in turn.

Staff development and retention

People development is especially important in executive protection. Solid training regimes are essential to program quality and are a key component in the ongoing effort to keep protective readiness high and complacency low. Likewise, critical but perishable skills that might be used rarely or never, such as CPR, must be consistently refreshed to be ready if called for.

Good agents, almost by definition, want to keep developing their skills. Programs with poor focus on training will lose these good agents more quickly than programs that build in regular training opportunities and demands. Some of the biggest in-house programs can and do provide excellent training, but many, especially small- and medium-sized programs, don't. Of course, this is also the case for the wide range of executive protection vendors; however, the incentives for these companies to focus on training — especially the best of them — are generally higher than for organizations for which executive protection isn't a core competency.

Many good agents (and, yes, some not as good ones) want to keep moving up the career ladder. A position as team lead can be a first step for some. A role as program manager might be a second move up, but for fewer. There are simply not as many programs out there as there are individuals who aspire to lead them. Lateral moves might also be attractive at some points in a career, such as transitioning from a role as a residential agent to a travel team agent, or vice versa. Unfortunately, most in-house programs don't offer the scope and diversity of positions that make either vertical or horizontal career moves possible. The only way to move up or over is to find another job. The risks of high staff churn must be considered, but so must the risks of too-low staff churn: the people willing to stay in jobs despite the lack of career development opportunities aren't always the ones who perform best.

There are examples of in-house teams that address these potential problems beautifully; however, these are usually very large teams with years of trial-and-error experience, better-than-average funding, and outstanding management.

Termination of employment

It's important that corporate executive protection agents can be taken off the team immediately if something as simple — and unpredictable — as personal chemistry with the principal is not optimal.

Even very large corporate EP programs can almost never reassign an agent asked to leave one position to another part of the protection team. Likewise, it's extremely improbable the corporation can find work for a dismissed EP expert in another part of the business. The consequence for the corporation is that the agent should be fired, which can be both difficult and costly.

Salary Cost Breakdown

Cost	Level 1	Level 2	Level 3
Agent Salary	80,000	100,000	120,000
Recruitment Costs (advertising, hiring, interviewing, management time, screening, and training)	3,865	3,865	3,865
Agent benefits (bonus, health, PTO, de minimus, etc. Salary x 30%)	24,000	30,000	36,000
Payroll Taxes	6,120	7,650	9,180
Training	10,000	10,000	10,000
Screening/ background testing	500	500	500
Certifications/licenses	1,000	1,000	1,000
Insurance	1,500	1,500	1,500
Technology/equipment/ subscriptions	10,000	10,000	10,000
Total	**136,985**	**164,515**	**192,045**

An article by the Society for Human Resource Management, *The Cost of a Bad Hire Can Be Astronomical*[3], reports that direct and indirect termination costs can be as high as $240,000. In addition to severance packages, the article cites such expenses as:

- Recruitment advertising fees and staff time
- Relocation and training fees for replacement hires
- Negative impact on team performance
- Disruption to incomplete projects
- Outplacement services
- Weakened employer brand
- Litigation fees

Finally, an important note on costs concerns distinguishing between what the company pays and what the principal or family office pays. Are the executive protection services to be paid for by the client company, or will the principal pay for some of the costs, for example, those that cover residen-tial protection or protection of the principal's family members?

Often, the answer is both. This can present the corporation with accounting challenges and lead to gaps in security for the principal. The utilization of a specialist partner provides seamless protection services regardless of whether the corporation or its employee is footing the bill. Costs can be more easily segregated between business and personal use when services are provided by a specialist partner.

How do the performance and quality of in-house executive protection teams compare against outsourced teams?

Specialist partners are, well, specialists. The best of them have management teams with hands-on executive protection experience that can be decades long. They have quality management systems and operating procedures that have proven their worth in practice. They know how to recruit and develop agents who go on to have success. And they can transfer skills learned working for one corporation to another. Admittedly, the worst of them don't and most lie somewhere in between.

Unlike in-house programs that build their capabilities on their own — and sometimes in isolated silos — pure-play, specialist partners that serve many clients can and often must benchmark against other programs. Companies with many clients are more likely to have a hard-earned sense of what constitutes best industry practices and to bring this to their clients in many ways, from program design and implementation to full or partial staffing and quality control.

Specialist partners can also enable speedy implementation and adaptation. Good specialist partners can implement viable protection programs in less than 48 hours, something that would take months for an inexperienced corporation or family office to do. Given the backdrop of why we do what we do — often tangible threats to the principal's well-being — fast program implementation can be a necessity, not a luxury.

Furthermore, good specialist partners can be better than in-house teams at adapting to evolving program needs. They've tried many things before, and they understand predictable pitfalls and opportunities. Should the program need to be scaled up, domestically or internationally, to cover other principals or to provide more protection in more places, this can be done without lengthy onboarding and training processes. Depending on the vendor, other services such as event security, secure travel logistics, and intelligence analysis can often be added immediately.

Similarly, if the program should need to be scaled back for whatever reason, then this can be done straight away and without concern for termination costs.

What are the risks of setting up your own corporate executive protection program?

From a security perspective, the most important risk associated with in-sourcing or outsourcing executive protection is poor performance of the protective team. Should the team fail to do its job properly, the consequences can, in the extreme, be catastrophic for the principal, their family, the company, and its shareholders. Other risks related to in-sourcing or outsourcing corporate executive protection fall into two broad categories: the ever-present risk of litigation, especially but not only in the US, and personnel risks. Both matter.

The intersection of human nature and corporate politics presents other real risks to executive protection programs. Executive protection is by its very nature up close and personal. Relationships between the principal and protective staff matter. Understanding the relational hazards of executive protection programs, including favoritism, significantly reduces the risk of program hiccups and failure. Favoritism of one agent over others leads to overreliance on that agent, bigheadedness, and eventual burnout. The risk is real, and inexperienced corporate departments are more likely to run into it than seasoned specialist partners.

Because protection agents spend a lot of time in the immediate proximity of the principal, small things can have a large impact. Personality traits and mannerisms aren't necessarily right or wrong. Still, personality is plenty of reason to ask for another protective agent, or even to dismiss one. If the principal becomes dissatisfied with a manager or agent for whatever reason, this might compromise the program and the principal's security and productivity. It's therefore imperative that the principal not hesitate, due to respect for the executive protection agent's feelings or corporate HR practices, to initiate termination of a person with whom they're uncomfortable. This is easier to do in outsourced programs and more likely to happen in a timely way.

Since principals often spend more time with executive protection agents than with their senior management team (and always more time than with the corporation's security director or chief security officer) agents' positions can carry perceived vicarious power. Agents must be of a special psychological makeup to handle such a role. It can be unfair to put an employee in that situation. Specialist partners have better conditions for handling this sensitive situation than corporate employees because they must treat everyone in the client organization as a customer — not just the CEO. This encourages cooperation and harmony rather than favoritism, bigheadedness, and rivalry.

If Insourcing Executive Protection Rarely Makes Objective Sense, Why Does It Occur?

To sum up the above, there are few good business or tactical arguments in favor of insourcing executive protection. Still, it happens all the time, especially but not only in large, complex programs. Why? I'm not privy to the discussions that lead to insourcing decisions, so I couldn't tell you the exact reasons, but I believe the motivation for most insourcing has to do with three issues.

Company culture

If you run any number of other make-or-buy decisions through the criteria employed above, you'll discover that many (most?) non-critical services, objectively, should be outsourced. However, in some cases, they aren't. This is true for standalone services like canteens, cleaning, and guarding; it might also apply to parts of other broader business functions like finance, HR, or marketing.

In some organizations, that's just how it is. "We want all employees to feel like they're part of the Acme Corp family, so even our canteen staff and security guards are FTEs."

In other organizations, that's how it is . . . until it isn't. New managers bring new ideas. The pendulum swings. Insourced services get outsourced, and outsourced services get insourced. All the good arguments you heard a few years ago are no longer good. But don't throw them away, because they might be useful again in another few years.

Company culture doesn't necessarily have to make objective sense. But it does explain many otherwise inscrutable decisions.

Perceived loyalty

Because protective staff are in close proximity to CEOs and founders, they might see and hear things that are sensitive to the business in general and the principal in particular. Discretion is key and loyalty is a must. Wouldn't our own FTEs be more reliable than those of a vendor?

Maybe. Maybe not. In my experience, the main thing in this connection is personal integrity, not employment status. I imagine there are just as many (if not more) tell-all-tales by butt-hurt bodyguards directly hired by their principals than there are by butt-hurt vendors.

Worries about staff turnover

Staff churn creates real challenges for program continuity. Isn't it easier to retain our own FTEs than it is to keep vendor staff onboard?

Again, this might sometimes be the case, but usually isn't. If you examine the actual reasons for executive protection staff quitting or getting fired, who's paying their salary isn't anywhere near the top of the list. On the contrary, people quit jobs primarily due to poor management here and better career opportunities elsewhere. They get fired because of things like poor performance and personal chemistry.

Converting contractors to employees: Try before you buy

A common reason for employee attrition in executive protection companies is rarely discussed openly: Agents and managers working for contractors get hired by the client organization. This is also referred to as "employee poaching" or, more formally, "contract-to-direct-hire conversion." Within executive protection, this phenomenon occurs in large, complex programs and smaller, simpler contexts alike.

Over the years, I've seen this happen many times. Instead of complaining about it, I decided long ago to accept it as a fact of life. As mentioned above, organizations have their reasons for insourcing, and it's not my place to argue with company culture or perceptions of loyalty. Agents and managers who make the change are usually motivated by perceptions of job security and benefits such as stock options, but some also see an opportunity to move up the career ladder or simply make a change. Whether or not "converted" employees end up more secure in their employment or are able to make any money on their options can be difficult to predict (and I don't argue one way or another). I don't try to convince people who want to make a move to stay.

I do, however, recommend that organizations that are considering insourcing their protection programs — or even just parts of it — "try before they buy." Generally speaking, outsourcing a program for at least a year gives an organization that's new to executive protection much better insight into what it is, what it means to principals, and why it works or doesn't. This understanding will prevent some of the typical beginner problems. Client companies that "convert" individual vendor employees also have an opportunity to get to know people before hiring them.

How program complexity and maturity affect the make-or-buy decision

Given all of the above, it might surprise some readers that I believe insourcing can also work just fine. While it might not be the rule, there are successful exceptions — some of which with I've been personally involved. Generally speaking, however, this holds true only for large, complex programs. The far more numerous smaller/simpler executive protection programs are better off outsourcing everything. Why?

- **Quality management:** Small programs generally don't comprise an executive protection manager but only agents, vehicles, and drivers. Compared to good external vendors, simple and small in-house programs run by the corporation or family office itself are very unlikely to have any kind of reliable quality management systems.

- **Silo mentality:** In these smaller programs, in which networking with other protection practitioners is rare, the likelihood of silo mentality is strong. Inherent to isolated groups, such silo mentality can easily lead to poor readiness and satisfaction with mediocre practices.

In this context, it's important to recall that all large and complex in-house programs are, strictly speaking, hybrid programs. They might employ their own managers and some or most of their own agents, but they invariably rely on vendors for at least some tasks — whether it's supplemental agents, security drivers and vehicles while traveling, or perhaps highly specialized protective intelligence analysts, remote operation center staff, or some other outsourced service. Furthermore, large, complex programs often utilize "embedded" staff who work exclusively at the client's locations, are legally employed by a vendor, and can have dotted or solid lines to the vendor's own managers or managers employed by the client.

Embedding executive protection agents and managers (and, in complex programs, other roles e.g., intelligence analysts) has its own advantages. These people live and breathe in the corporate ecosystem, but also have the benefits of being able to draw on the specialist partner's network of expertise. Fully mature, large, complex executive protection programs are often a hybrid of own full-time employees, employees embedded from a specialist partner, and other vendor employees working on a more ad hoc basis.

Understanding program complexity

Program complexity can be approached in many ways. In the context of sourcing decisions, I propose a simple model that views complexity as a function of both the principals' risk profile and where and how frequently they receive protective coverage.

Below, two fictive scenarios illustrate how this model can provide a workable measure of complexity (see the **Key   on page   99**). Of course, determining risk levels is a process all its own, and other parameters can be added, but I believe the model gives a useful perspective that can help answer the insourcing/outsourcing question more clearly.

Scenario A			
Location	Risk Level	Frequency	SCORE
Fixed site — Residential	3	5	**15**
Fixed site — Office/ campus			
Fixed site — Event	3	2	**6**
Driving — Travel — foreign and domestic			
Driving — Local — commute home-office			
Driving — Local — other			
Travel — Foreign	3	2	**6**
Travel — Domestic			
Mobile/ walking — Work			
Mobile/ walking — Private			
Mobile/ walking — Covert			
TOTAL SCORE			27

Scenario B				
	Location	Risk Level	Frequency	SCORE
Fixed Site	Residential	4	5	20
Fixed Site	Office/ campus	2	5	10
Fixed Site	Event	4	5	20
Driving	Travel — foreign and domestic	4	3	12
Driving	Local — commute home-office	4	5	20
Driving	Local — other	4	5	20
Travel	Foreign	4	4	16
Travel	Domestic	4	4	16
Mobile/ Walking	Work	2	2	4
Mobile/ Walking	Private	4	5	20
Mobile/ Walking	Covert	4	5	20
TOTAL SCORE				178

Key			
Risk Level		**Frequency**	
1	Low	1	Ad hoc
2	Low-medium	2	Sometimes
3	Medium	3	Medium
4	High-medium	4	Usually
5	High	5	Always
Risk Level x Frequency = SCORE			

Scenario A represents a small, simple program. The principal's risk level is considered "medium," and coverage isn't very frequent but limited to some full-time residential agents, occasional event security, and protective support to some foreign destinations.

Conversely, Scenario B depicts a much bigger and more complex program. The principal's risk level is higher — though still not maximum — and the situations in which they receive coverage are far more numerous.

As outlined above, I'd be hard-pressed to recommend insourcing any part of Scenario A. The complexity does not justify it in any way, and the risks of poor quality and silo thinking are too great.

The situation is different for Scenario B. Here, there would definitely be a full-time program manager and several team leads employed as well as dozens of other FTEs. While vendors' cars and drivers would certainly be used for all foreign and most domestic travel, staffing the rest of the program could easily be a mix of in-house and outsourced employees. Should most of this staff be in-house or vendor-employed? I believe the objective arguments would favor outsourcing most if not all of these positions. However, in the real world of different company cultures, perceptions of loyalty, and expectations regarding staff churn, there are all kinds of variation between the poles of pure outsourced and predominantly insourced. How well these multi-faceted programs work depends more on the quality of the management and the people/processes/technology involved than it does on who employs whom.

Program Maturity Also Affects Make-or-Buy Decisions

The relative maturity of the protective program also affects insourcing/outsourcing decisions.

Most principals start using executive protection in a small way. This could be some kind of residential security staff or protective coverage for selected events and travel destinations. In some cases, such arrangements go on for a long time without evolving into anything more. In other cases, the ad hoc projects become more regular, and other program components are gradually added. While there are instances of corporations and family offices using the "I got a guy" method, e.g., the part or full-time hiring of retired or off-duty law enforcement officers to supply any perceived coverage needs, many principals typically outsource these new protection services rather than hire their own part- or full-time staff. Additional complexity might bring changes in how these services are sourced.

New programs that provide more comprehensive executive protection are often 100 percent outsourced initially. When comprehensive security needs are sudden, only specialist partners can get a program up to speed quickly. Corporate security departments have neither the expertise nor other resources to establish the program on its own. Engagement of vendors in these cases typically includes consulting on program setup, outsourcing executive protection agents and/or residential security agents, and often outsourcing an executive protection manager.

As the program matures, the corporation may choose to make the executive protection manager its first full-time protection employee. This could be with or without consulting support from a specialist partner. Insourcing the program manager squarely places the executive protection function on the corporation's organizational chart, establishes the function as a corporate priority, and enables the corporate executive protection manager to be a fully integrated part of the corporation's security setup. Some organizations stop insourcing here, others continue to hire some or all executive protection and residential security agents.

Key Takeaways	
This chapter examines the relative advantages and disadvantages of in-sourcing and outsourcing executive protection services	
1	Those responsible should consider the four basic criteria and associated questions: • **Core competencies** Are the competencies necessary to deliver the services core to the corporation's strategy and success? • **Cost efficiency** What are the total costs of making or buying the given service — and how do they compare? • **Performance capability** How difficult is it to develop the necessary capabilities? Can an insourced program deliver the same quality and perform as well as best-in-class industry leaders? • **Risks** What are the risks associated with either insourcing or outsourcing the service?
2	Although there are rarely strong business or tactical reasons to insource executive protection, it's often considered due to questions of company culture, perceived loyalty, and worries about staff turnover.
3	Program complexity and maturity also affect make-or-buy decisions. Generally, simpler and less mature programs are better off outsourcing, while in-sourcing is most relevant for large, mature programs. Program complexity can be understood with the help of a simple model that views complexity as a function of both the principals' risk profile and where and how frequently they receive protective coverage.

Section 1 Endnotes

1 Fein, Robert A., and Bryan Vossekuil. *Preventing Assassination: Secret Service Exceptional Case Study Project.* Publication no. 167224, National Contest Journal, 1 Jan. 1997.

2 Pichère, Pierre, and Anne-Christine Cadiat. *Maslow's Hierarchy of Needs.* Lemaitre, 2015.

3 Frye, Lisa. "The Cost of a Bad Hire Can Be Astronomical." *The Society for Human Resource Management*, 9 May 2017, www.shrm.org/topics-tools/news/employee-relations/cost-bad-hire-can-astronomical.

SECTION 2:
Managing the Executive Protection Program

If Larry was good enough for the Secret Service, he's good enough for Acme Corp.

Larry seemed the perfect match when Acme Corp hired its first director of executive protection. He had years of military experience, where he served as an intelligence officer and did several tours in Afghanistan. A black belt in karate, he looked the part and still won competitions in his age class. But it was his career at the Secret Service, where he worked his way up from a special agent to a management position in an intelligence department, that really set him apart from the other applicants.

The CSO that hired him didn't have any direct experience with executive protection but was not in doubt. He checked in with two other CSOs to get some pointers on setting up a new EP program, and one of them had hired a candidate with extensive government experience, too. Given the new EP director's background, there had been little trouble getting the hire approved internally: If Larry was good enough to work for the US Secret Service, which among many other duties protected the US president, then he was more than capable to head up Acme Corp's executive protection program for its CEO.

Acme Corp's EP program was in definite need of a good manager. It had grown quickly in fewer than than 18 months and the time had come for the corporation to set up its own program rather than depend on the ex-state police officer and various vendors who had handled things until then.

Extra security had begun when the CEO received threats after activists publicized how many laboratory animals the pharma company used every year. Things got worse when a new blockbuster drug the company launched was criticized first for the drug's high price, then for its unintended side effects. The corporation's and the CEO's media mentions and appearances grew as steadily as sales. When uninvited "guests" started showing up at the CEO's home and frightening his family, Acme Corp posted a few security guards at the residence. All the CSO needed to do was ask the guard company that had the contract for the corporation's headquarters and production facilities to add some shifts at the CEO's place. After several incidents led to the CEO getting protection at events, the CSO hired the former state police officer to escort the CEO on some occasions, and to contract with off-duty police officers to provide protection at others. When he traveled domestically and abroad, the CEO's executive assistant (EA) booked bespoke limousine services for him and hired security agents for some destinations if that was considered necessary.

In just a year and a half, what was once the occasional extra security had morphed into a protective hodgepodge. Several board members with experience from other corporations raised the issue, and the CSO was tasked with creating a more comprehensive program. He quickly decided to organize all these efforts under one manager who would be Acme Corp's first director of executive protection.

Larry was headhunted through the CSO's network. His first move was to work with procurement to develop an RFP for a program that included protection at the principal's main residence, at the corporate campus, and for all travel. Four well-known executive protection companies were invited to submit proposals. With the active participation of the CSO and procurement, Larry helped select a vendor with extensive experience and an impressive roster of current and past corporate clients.

There were plenty of early wins for Larry. After some initial hiccups Larry tackled with his hands-on, no-nonsense approach honed by years in the government, the vendor made some changes and began performing closer to Larry's expectations. In time, the principal accepted the presence of agents in his professional and personal spheres. As the program included security drivers for his daily commute and most travel, the principal began to appreciate the time he spent in vehicles as a chance to prepare for meetings, catch up with people he had to talk to, or zone out for a while if that's what he needed. Some of the agents were pretty nice guys that the principal and his family had warmed up to. Larry had the backing of his CSO and was hitting his KPIs, and the principal seemed happy enough.

Not everyone was thrilled with Larry's style, however. The EAs who worked on the C-suite floor were fiercely loyal to the CEO and protected his time and productivity like hawks. They appreciated Larry and his team organizing security instead of them but were increasingly put off by what they perceived as his abrasive demeanor. Larry needed them to provide information about the CEO's travel destinations, itineraries, and meetings, and they were happy to comply. But Larry's way of ordering this information rather than asking for it, of treating them as subordinates rather than equal-footed colleagues, and often getting upset when last-minute changes to plans occurred, which they inevitably did, rubbed the EAs the wrong way.

They continued to provide information on the boss's comings and goings as best they could, but even simple conversations became tense when plans changed in the eleventh-hour. Larry thought they were withholding information to make him look bad, and he let them know as much. The EAs, who had all worked long hours for Acme Corp for years, shared their growing frustration with Larry with the principal, who complained to the CFO, to whom the CSO reported. By that time, the situation had devolved into "us or him." Needless to say, he left, and the CSO was soon on the lookout for a new director of executive protection.

Chapter 2-1:

The executive protection ecosystem in corporate settings

Culture Eats Strategy for Breakfast

Executive protection managers working for corporations would do well to remember the words of management guru Peter Drucker: "Company cultures are like country cultures. Never try to change one. Try, instead, to work with what you've got."

Because no matter what an executive protection manager may have learned in the military, government, or law enforcement, working in a modern corporation is different in so many ways. Let's examine a few of them:

- **Structure:** In corporations, the vertical hierarchies common to the military and governments are replaced by the matrix organization, where one person may have multiple reporting lines and loyalties, and conflicts of interest are common.

- **Rules of conduct:** Proper behavior is more implied or understood than defined by explicit rules.

- **Rank and status:** While rank is clearly marked and understood in the military, those with influence in corporations aren't always identifiable by their titles.

- **Career progression:** Unlike the military's clear career ladder, corporate employees have a varied career flow. Lateral job changes in a matrix organization can bring significant changes to one's career.

If corporate executive protection managers and agents are going to have success, then they need to understand that corporate cultures all vary and that no two corporations are alike.

For one thing, there are significant differences between industries. Just look at how cultures in tech start-ups differ from pharmaceutical or oil and gas companies. However, there are significant company differences within the same industries, too. To thrive, executive protection professionals must have an excellent understanding of the corporation's mission, values, beliefs, power structures, stories, myths . . . and everything else that underpins corporate culture.

Navigating the Organizational Chart: Know Your Stakeholders

Corporate executive protection managers are typically tasked with protecting one or more C-level principals. But this doesn't mean the principal is the only individual with whom they need to develop working relationships.

On the contrary, successful executive protection managers need to know all of the many stakeholders in corporate executive protection and establish strong collaborative relationships throughout the ecosystem. Most stakeholder analyses will include the following persons and departments or their equivalents.

Executive administrative assistants to the principal

For protection providers, the executive administrative assistant (EAA) to the principal is the (second) most important stakeholder in the entire organization.

Both gateway and gatekeeper, the EAA has all the information on the principal's meeting and travel schedules: the bread-and-butter information around which so much protective planning depends. As schedules often change — sometimes at the last minute — having an open line to the EAA is essential.

The EAA is, furthermore, the main communication channel between the executive protection manager and the principal. Not only does the EAA keep the protective team informed of the principal's comings and goings, but they're also the one who is most likely to get direct feedback from the principal about the executive protection team and then send it on — or not. For example, the EAA might know that the principal was unhappy with an agent's behavior before anyone else. Program managers want to be the next one to know — not the last — so they can take appropriate action.

But EAAs also play another important role in corporate executive protection. In frequent contact with the protective team, they can be powerful allies in helping principals and other corporate stakeholders understand what the executive protection team does and why it needs to do it. As such, the EAA's understanding of executive protection is invaluable, and it would behoove all corporate team members to facilitate and deepen this understanding. For example, knowing that the executive protection team needs to conduct advance work for trips allows the EAA to plan trip itineraries accordingly. Sometimes a little understanding goes a long way in smoothing out the inevitable frictions that arise in fast-paced corporate environments.

Partnership between the executive protection team and the EAA is essential given the many interdependencies between the two. When the relationship is good, it allows both parties to do their jobs well. For example, the executive protection team often functions as an extension of the EAA's office when the principal is on the road. Let's say the principal is traveling abroad and needs a presentation that a team back at HQ is working on up until the last minute before an important meeting in a hotel. The EAA can depend on the executive protection team to get the file by secure email, get it printed, and get it into the principal's hands within minutes — all while maintaining security and confidentiality. After all, it's the executive protection team who's traveling with the principal, knows the layout of the hotel, and can make secure arrangements with the business center — not the EAA.

A simple word of advice to protection managers: Never make the EAA say "I don't know" to the principal. Keep them informed of what you're doing, why you're doing it, who's on the team — and who's got the ball on all the important tasks.

Corporate communications/ public relations

Executive protection teams must also understand what corporate communications/public relations (PR) teams do and maintain an open and ongoing dialogue with them. Both parties have an interest in some of the same things, albeit often for different reasons. Let's take the principal's prominence as an example. PR professionals are tasked with building and maintaining corporate reputations as well as those of their key principals. Media prominence for the right things (and as few of the wrong things as possible) is an important goal for and result of their work.

For executive protection professionals, however, "increased prominence" often translates into "increased risk." We need to know about any plans and activities by corporate communications that can predictably increase our principal's prominence. Controversial topics can quickly turn into hot buttons for everyone from activists to anarchists. Rightly or wrongly, the principal immediately becomes the lightning rod for all kinds of people with all kinds of grief, and folks with an axe to grind might end up wielding the axe. Executive protection managers need to know what might bump up a principal's prominence prior to any major announcement, so they can plan accordingly.

Similarly, the executive protection team needs to learn from corporate communications how to handle the press. We never want to be part of the story, but we should be able to help journalists get theirs when possible and in accordance with a coordinated plan developed by the PR and executive protection teams.

Proper training and coordination can also enable frontline executive protection agents to redirect the press away from a principal and toward the appropriate contact. The result enhances security for the principal and gives journalists access to someone who can provide the information they're looking for.

Corporate travel

Executive protection managers must always maintain good relationships with the corporate travel department.

We move with the principal, frequently at short notice, and corporate travel employees are often the people who help us with air travel, short-notice visa applications, hotels, and many other practicalities.

Travel departments may have to bend corporate procedures to enable executive protection agents to do their jobs. If the principal is staying at the Four Seasons, then some of the executive protection team will also have to stay at the Four Seasons even though the price exceeds normal guidelines.

Executive protection agents who maintain good relationships with their counterparts in corporate travel are happy executive protection agents. It's not hard to do if you remember some of the things your mother tried to teach you: be nice, treat people with respect, and say please and thank you. And remember to apologize when you have to make them jump through hoops for you.

Legal

The executive protection team may need to consult with the legal department for a variety of reasons. First, use-of-force policies and practices must always be cleared with legal to mitigate the risk of litigation. Second, people of interest must be handled in a coordinated partnership, so the executive protection team (with the possible support from intelligence analysts) takes care of personal security, and legal takes care of relations with law enforcement if restraining orders are needed. If such a threat goes public, then corporate communications will also be part of the picture.

Finance

While executive protection may be a way of life for us in the industry, it's just another cost center for the bean counters. And a highly unpredictable one at that.

Fixed executive protection costs are not difficult to budget. However, many variable costs related to executive protection are activity-driven and were not known when budgets were originally written and approved.

This is especially true for travel. Unplanned trips happen all the time, and unexpected turns of events can add unbudgeted travel costs fast. Of course, it's in everyone's interest that executive protection teams keep their budgets, but when the security of the principal is at stake, we also want them to think fast and have their priorities in order. Sticking to the budget no matter what might be responsible behavior for a marketing department, but that's not necessarily the case for corporate executive protection.

Does that mean finance departments give executive protection teams carte blanche to run up expenses? Of course not. It does mean executive protection managers need to keep finance informed about unbudgeted expenses as they develop.

Human resources (HR)

Depending on how the corporate executive protection effort is organized, corporate HR may or may not be an important interface.

If the entire executive protection program is contracted, even if some of the team is embedded within the corporation, then all HR responsibility rests on the executive protection company, not on the principal's corporation.

If, on the other hand, some or all members of the executive protection team are full-time employees of the corporation, then the executive protection manager has an important reason to stay close to HR: Corporate HR departments rarely have any experience with the special career paths of an executive protection manager or agent, and they need help in recruiting, understanding how to evaluate performance, establishing job ladders and career planning, and all of the other things HR operations typically handle for other departments. See **Section 4: Managing Changes in Executive Protection Programs** to dig deeper into some of these issues.

Other security-related departments and vendors

Executive protection teams will have direct liaison with a number of other corporate functions and external vendors that also form part of corporate security efforts.

In some cases, these teams will be under the same management as the executive protection team. In others, reporting lines will be different. In any case, it's important that corporate executive protection teams build and maintain close partnerships with the following parties.

Physical security

As the protectors of the corporate grounds and all of its buildings, assets, and staff, security officers and the rest of the physical security team play a vital role in the overall, day-to-day protection of the corporation. In terms of protecting the principal, they also play a key role. They keep persons of interest (POIs) outside of the corporate campus and far away from the principal while they're within the corporate perimeter. Clear communication between the executive protection and physical security teams is crucial. The physical protection team doesn't necessarily know where the principal is; the executive protection team does. Good communication between the two teams can prevent or mitigate situations in which a breach of overall campus security can affect that of the personal security of the principal.

- **Security operations center (SOC):** Both the physical protection teams and the executive protection teams might share the same hub through which they coordinate corporate and personal security.
- **Security technology resources:** Similarly, both teams will ideally have access to the same technologies (e.g., video feeds, building entrance and exit data) that enable them to do their jobs.

Intelligence analysts

Analysts may or may not be an integrated part of the executive protection team. In any case, regular communication between executive protection and analysts is an important part of keeping the principal secure. Executive protection relies on intelligence to discover and keep an eye on emerging threats and persons of interest. We also depend on intelligence for updates on countries and cities where we will be traveling with the principal, so we can prepare and plan accordingly.

Family offices

Corporate principals will often maintain a family office to manage the family's personal financial, philanthropic, or other affairs (see **Chapter 2-2** for more on family offices). Spouses or other family members of the principal are often involved. The executive protection team must also keep communication lines to the family office open and clear. Travel and social commitments that originate within the family office must be coordinated with those of the corporation, so the executive protection team can provide seamless protection of the principal and their family as required.

Estate management

The executive protection manager must also coordinate closely with estate managers and staff on matters like background checks for nannies and other staff and check-in processes for guests and service personnel.

External vendors and contractors

Corporate executive protection managers depend on external suppliers to supplement their own teams as needs arise. For example, few US corporations have the need or capacity to maintain their own vetted drivers in Latin America, even though their principals might need to travel there occasionally or even frequently. The executive protection manager relies instead on external secure transportation providers. By working with a lead supplier for secure transportation or embedded executive protection agents, an executive protection manager can increase responsiveness and scale up or down rapidly as needs change.

Communication Is Key

Consistent, effective communication between the executive protection team and other parts of the corporate executive protection ecosystem is what sets successful programs apart from failures.

Put simply, it's all about doing your job and helping other people in the organization to do theirs. A good understanding of the organization helps protection vendors to engage with the proper cross-organizational resources proactively rather than creating extra work and frustration. Similarly, a good understanding of the executive protection effort enables others in the organization to contribute to it.

It's the responsibility of the executive protection manager to communicate openly and clearly to other corporate stakeholders about many issues, including:

- The purpose of the executive protection program
- The importance of an ongoing RTVA mindset as the foundation of protecting the principal
- Mutual understanding and shared views of standard executive protection operating procedures (without getting into the operational weeds)
- Operational follow-up and reporting

Regular, face-to-face meeting with key stakeholders is important. With some, such as the EAA, these meetings may be weekly. With others, they may be monthly or quarterly. Whatever the frequency, the executive protection manager needs to address all relevant issues openly.

Documentation of activities and recommendations is crucial to enable others to understand how executive protection works. Make sure that it goes upward within your chain of command and to other key stakeholders.

In a corporate setup that isn't familiar with executive protection, the executive protection manager will often have to explain the value and importance of specific executive protection activities. Recommendations should be backed by data and rational arguments. Rather than using military jargon or processes that protectors may be familiar with, recommendations should be framed in a way that's familiar to the corporation.

In addition to explaining executive protection to corporate stakeholders who may not be familiar with its thinking and procedures, good documentation leaves a trail we can revisit in case something goes wrong, allowing us to learn from mistakes and continually improve our corporate executive protection programs.

Key Takeaways	
1	Executive protection managers and agents must understand, adapt to, and work within existing organizational cultures, not try to change them.
2	Many stakeholders interact with and impact executive protection providers in different ways. Ensure program success by knowing who they are and establishing good communication and strong collaborative relationships with: • Executive administrative assistants (EAAs) to the principal • Corporate communications/public relations • Corporate travel • Legal • Finance • Human resources (HR)
3	You should also establish these relationships with other security-related departments and vendors, including: • Physical security • Security operations centers (SOCs) • Security technology resources • Intelligence analysts • Family offices • Estate management • External vendors and contractors

Chapter 2-2:

As Leo Tolstoy pointed out, happy families are alike, but unhappy families are all unhappy in their own ways. We believe the Anna Karenina principle applies to the protection of high-net-worth families, too. But only if we turn it on its head:

> Successful high-net-worth family protection programs are all different, but unsuccessful programs usually fail for the same reasons.

In this chapter, I'll examine the ecosystem of high-net-worth protection programs to understand the reasons why they succeed — and hopefully prevent program failure for more families.

The Four Keys to Success

To achieve success in high-net-worth family protection, it's important to understand the ecosystems in which security services are provided for these families and individuals. These ecosystems comprise many different dynamics and stakeholders, the security team being only one part of a larger whole. All families are different, of course, and so are the ways the many interacting parts of a complex network operate together.

Customization

Tailoring security to family culture and preferences starts with lots of questions and careful listening

Even executives who are used to some kind of protective services on the job can find home and family security bothersome at best and downright intrusive at worst. Putting up with outsiders at work is one thing. Having them close to family and friends at all times of the day is something else.

In our experience, the first step to a successful program is understanding the necessity of adapting security to the family's culture and individual preferences rather than the other way around. High-net-worth families are used to lots of customization options when it comes to many other aspects of their lives, and security should be no different. Neglecting to customize security practices to the family's individual needs and wants is a key cause of program failure. Everyone on the risk management stakeholder matrix introduced in **Chapter 1-2** would do well to remember this.

While we're all for watertight SOPs based on best practices, in reality these cannot simply be copy and pasted from one program to another. They need to be adapted to every new situation, especially when concerning the private sphere. And the best way to understand a family's culture and preferences is to stop talking and start listening. Paradoxically, among the many skills protection experts need to develop, active listening to genuinely understand client wishes ranks among the most difficult to master for many otherwise competent protectors.

Strangers at the gate and inside the walls: How does the family feel about having a residential security team on the property? And does the risk warrant it?

Bringing strangers into the inner sanctum of the home (even if they're there to protect and are very professional) tests the personal boundaries of any family. This can be especially difficult for people new to security. The best way to deal with this issue is openly. Put the issues on the table, make transparent the pros and cons of different alternatives, and ask questions.

- Is the family open to on-property security? To what extent and how?
- Can the residential security team roam the property to check up on things when time allows? When in the day?
- Do we need to stick to predefined routes, or can we do random patrols?
- Are there areas that are off-limits to security, where the family insists on total privacy?
- If the family does not want security on the property, do we park on the street? Can we rent a house or apartment next door?

False alarm: What kinds of physical security equipment are used for security, and does the use of this equipment match the way the family lives?

Alarms, sensors, and cameras are great security tools, but only if they get used. And they only get used if they're convenient and designed around the family's lifestyle and preferences. Cookie-cutter solutions that get tacked on to homes and family habits often end up being more bothersome than helpful, so they don't even get turned on. Instead of starting with prescriptions, it's important to ask questions.

For example:

- How does the family use their current system? How does the equipment match their daily habits? How do family members typically greet guests — at the door or with a security camera? What would a parent actually do if they were awakened by an alarm in the middle of the night? Where would they go first?
- Is the family OK with cameras? Where is it OK to record and where is simple observation all that is allowable? What do we need to mask out as sensitive areas due to privacy?
- What are the needs of all family members, spouses, and young or teenage children? What about safety around pools and play areas?

For high-net-worth families that have security teams at their residences, it's important to remember the tech is there to help the security team and should be run by them — not by the family. Basically, the tech should be seen as the team's extended eyes and ears, covering areas that team members do not, for one reason or another, cover with other team members or staff.

Larger, more complex protective teams will monitor all tech and provide other back-up services from an operations center. Whether this operations center is on the property or off depends, again, on the family's preferences as well as the property's physical layout.

Cooperation, not competition: What's the best way to align residential and other security elements?

While residential security is typically a big part of high-net-worth security, it's not the only one. Security drivers and executive protection also play a role in many programs, and it's important that all the pieces mesh together seamlessly as working parts of the security master plan. Again, asking open questions to better understand the family's preferences is critical.

- How do family members feel about driving? What about spouses and teenage children?
- Do they want to drive themselves or are security drivers needed for some or all trips?
- If principals do drive themselves, then are discreet security escorts an option?
- What about security driving skills training for them and GPS tracking?
- Do any of the family members use executive protection sometimes or always?

If there's an executive protection team, then it's critical to understand its role, too, and to coordinate this with the other pieces of the security master plan. Administrative issues are one thing, as the executive protection team might be paid for and managed through the principal's corporation and separately from the residential team. Security issues are another thing. Whether the executive protection teams operate covertly or overtly, seamless protection is only possible when residential and executive protection teams cooperate closely — and understand exactly when and how handoffs take place.

Communication

High-net-worth family security doesn't happen in a vacuum, so you must know your stakeholders and communicate effectively with them

The ecosystems of high-net-worth family security comprise far more stakeholders than the family and protection professionals. To be successful, everyone on the security team must first understand all stakeholder roles and agendas, and then respect and accommodate other stakeholders' needs as they go about their jobs.

Let's look at the main stakeholder categories and how they interact with protective security teams.

Family offices

Family offices help run the financial affairs and investments of many high-net-worth families. They also often help oversee the management of properties and may be directly or indirectly involved in hiring and liaising with security providers. There are two different configurations that you can encounter here — the single-family office and the multi-family office.

Security managers

Security managers must work closely with family offices on all financial and administrative issues, of course, but it's also important to keep them in the loop on all critical issues relating to program design and performance. Principals will often go through the family office when they want changes in their security, so it's key that family office managers, who are often our "clients," have excellent insight into what we're doing and why, and any HR issues are shared with them in an open and timely way. Regular meetings to review administrative and other issues are highly recommended.

Estate management and staff

Estate management, which is responsible for the day-to-day operations of one or more residences, may or may not be part of the family office. In any case, estate management is a close working partner of estate security and must be treated as such. Estate management and staff are the stakeholders that residential security teams interact with most frequently, so smooth cooperation is essential.

This is an area in which the security team must do its job and help others be successful in doing theirs. The protection team should aspire to be seen as an enabler and partner of the entire estate staff. While establishing boundaries is also important, creating trust and partnership among the family staff is paramount. This can be managed with clear, consistent communication as well as operational and financial transparency and an educational approach.

One area of collaboration is carrying out background checks for new staff hires. Another is developing and enforcing protocols for allowing craftspeople, caterers, and other commercial guests access to the property. There are many more.

Security professionals need to understand that estate staff often have relationships with the principal family that go way back and can be intensely loyal. Cleaning personnel and gardeners may have been with the family for years or even generations. Young nannies might well be trusted more than a seasoned security manager with a black belt and military distinctions.

> Like all other stakeholders in the high-net-worth ecosystem, everyone on the estate staff — everyone — must be treated with the utmost respect, always.

Private aircraft and yacht/maritime staff

Traveling teams such as air and yacht crew often have intel about upcoming family plans before anyone else in the ecosystem.

Intelligence Analysts

Intelligence analysts may be tasked with understanding threats posed by persons or groups of interest or other factors. They might also be involved in monitoring online activities related to the principals, providing travel intelligence, and other analyses.

Finally, it's important to remember that everyone throughout the ecosystem can also be considered as part of the overall protective effort. Excellent collaboration between security professionals and others working in the household runs deep as well as wide.

Everyone can benefit from security awareness training, for example, whether it's housekeepers, gardeners, or the principal's spouse and children. Nannies with security driver training are much safer in traffic than those who haven't received any special training. Fire safety and response training is relevant for all. And while tactical medical training should be required for security agents, other household staff members might be able to save lives if they, too, are properly trained.

Good security providers who want to become preferred partners add value not only on their own but through working with everyone else in the ecosystem to raise the bar on comprehensive protective services.

Flexibility

Good family security programs that are flexibly based on a good understanding of stakeholder needs, professional team members, trust, and cooperation

Developing and implementing protection programs for families is different than doing so for corporate clients. Programs in corporate environments are structured, managed, and delivered in keeping with corporate practices. Processes are formalized in ways similar to other business practices; decisions are made according to well-defined criteria; hierarchies are pretty clear.

Families are different. Emotions, feelings, and personal relations matter in a different way, as do self-image and perceptions. That's not good or bad; that's just the reality of working in the context of the family. And security professionals need to get it.

Family programs must view all family members as principals — the spouse, children, parents, and even friends. The important thing to understand here is that protection teams will be addressing different cultures, sets of expectations, and financial arrangements — and that everything must be customized to match the family's preferences, not a corporation's.

Key differences concern family dynamics and planning. Family programs must generally be more flexible than corporate, more sensitive to emotional needs, and even more able to adapt quickly to changing plans. Team members need to be comfortable with even more gray areas and potentially less communication and information. Even more than in corporate environments, this requires team members who have rock-solid judgment, creative problem-solving skills, and good intuition. They need to be people who like working with and for other people — in addition to being tactically competent.

Trust is earned by sharing information and respecting confidentiality

The importance of developing strong, trusting relationships throughout the family ecosystem cannot be over emphasized. Everyone delivering support to the family, whether on the security team, in management, or the family office will have different levels of communication and kinds of interaction with family members. Sharing information, lessons learned, and best practices across these groups goes a long way in establishing security program success.

But information sharing comes with responsibility and requires a mature understanding of confidentiality. Everyone serving the family in one capacity or another has access to different types of information. Some in the ecosystem should and do have more access to family members than others, and information is often compartmentalized for a reason. Sensitivities about what should be shared with whom and when are critical.

The goal for the team is to develop trust with the family members and each other. There may be times when one group or person has more trust from the family members and will want to solidify their position with the family by not sharing information that should be shared with other parts of the ecosystem. This can set up power struggles that are frustrating and destructive — and never add value for the family or its protection. Professional managers are aware of this potentiality and work hard to create a team environment across the family ecosystem. Choosing team members and leaders who have mature interpersonal skills and can keep their egos in check are critical elements in hiring. Unfortunately, these character traits are often overlooked or underprioritized. There are many examples of executive protection agents and managers who were hired for their tactical skills and experience gained in government agencies or the military but fired because their "people skills" didn't go over well with private sector individuals and families.

Adaptability

Programs must readily adapt to changes in the ecosystem and evolving client needs — and make sure programs are ready to adapt

Finally, no matter how hard we work to establish a great family protection program, we must face the fact that this, too, will change.

Babies are born. Young adults go off to college and new jobs. Personal relationships begin, evolve, and end. Staff are hired and fired or move on for other reasons. And, of course, the risks, threats, and vulnerabilities that inform security measures are also ever-changing.

Successful family protection programs take a proactive approach to these dynamics. They focus on ongoing quality management and HR development, develop ways to combat team complacency, and boost responsiveness to client needs.

Key Takeaways	
Executive protection providers working for high-net-worth families must pay special attention to four distinct issues:	
1	**Customization** Tailoring security to family culture and preferences starts with lots of questions and careful listening.
2	**Communication** High-net-worth family security doesn't happen in a vacuum, so you must know your stakeholders and communicate effectively with them. These include family office staff, security managers, estate managers and staff, intelligence analysts, and private aircraft and yacht/maritime staff.
3	**Flexibility** Good family security programs are flexibly based on a good understanding of stakeholder needs, professional team members, trust, and cooperation.
4	**Adaptability** Programs must readily adapt to changes in the ecosystem and evolving client needs — and make sure programs are ready to adapt.

Chapter 2-3:

The overarching purpose of executive protection programs can be boiled down to a simple idea: mitigating risk to
the principal to an acceptable level. However, such a broad
statement of purpose is not operationally practical. Just as
"maximizing shareholder value" might be a good description of
a corporation's overall objectives, the goal is too broad to guide
the many managers who are responsible for making this happen.
Departmental goals need to be aligned with corporate goals, of
course, but they must also be specific enough to create results
on a daily basis.

So, the first responsibility of the corporate executive
protection manager is to define program objectives that are
clear and actionable to the executive protection team, the
principal, and all key players in the corporate or family office
ecosystems. Even when these goals pull in different directions,
good executive protection managers find creative ways to strike
a consistent, high-performing equilibrium among them all.

In this chapter, I'll introduce four overall objectives that
apply to practically any executive protection program. Specific
program objectives should then build on and expand these high-
level goals.

Match Program Deliveries to an Ongoing Analysis of a Principal's Profile and the Resulting Risks, Threats, and Vulnerabilities

Whether they like it or not, executive protection principals are often public figures who get a lot of media attention. Their prominence can in fact be higher than that of politicians or celebrities with significant name recognition — people with whom they would never compare themselves otherwise.

When setting objectives, executive protection managers must consider the principal's prominence profile as well as any events or changes that could impact that profile. This could be anything from an initial public offering to a family matter or a controversial tweet. It's important the RTVA isn't a static document that was written and then placed in a drawer. To be truly useful in an ever-changing world, the RTVA must be a dynamic process that continually assesses as many factors as is feasible.

Conceive and Implement the Program According to Best-Practice Executive Protection Standards

Continuous operational excellence is a key objective of any executive protection program, and it's the responsibility of the executive protection manager to ensure that the team performs accordingly.

To do this, the executive protection manager must establish SOPs according to industry best practices for all team activities, as well as all metrics and KPIs to ensure these are kept. These procedures must cover all aspects of protection, from advance work to after-action reviews.

Of course, all of this must take place within the boundaries of the available budget. If budgetary constraints impinge on the manager's ability to deliver best-in-class protection, then the manager will have to lobby for more resources — and at the same time find creative ways to work within the budget.

The Protective Circle can be useful here, too. It encourages managers to comprehensively set goals and measure performance in all relevant aspects of existing programs, and it points the way to improving programs by closing protective gaps.

Align the Program with Corporate or Family Objectives, Practices, and Culture

Because executive protection sometimes fits like a round peg into the square hole of usual routines, it's especially impor-tant that the executive protection manager aligns the program with the corporation's and/or family's way of doing things. In order to deliver against this objective, the executive protection manager must have good answers to multiple questions.

- What are the rules and policies — written and unwritten — that affect the program?
- Which values, norms, and shared assumptions make it easy to provide executive protection — and which make it difficult?
- How does one best navigate through the organization's formal structures and unofficial power relationships?

We often tell new agents working on an executive protection team that one objective is "don't make the principal think." By this, we mean that executive protection agents need to fit naturally within the organization's or family's normal way of doing things, aka its culture. For example, saying "Good morning, sir" in an organization where everyone is on a first-name basis with the CEO creates a cumbersome moment that makes the principal think, "Who is this guy?" instead of simply going about his business. We're there to facilitate business, not get in its way.

Carry out the Program According to the Principal's Personal Preferences

Although a principal's lifestyle choices are unlikely to have any effect on corporate or family office accounting procedures, they make a world of difference to the practice of executive protection. Unless the principal's personal preferences are included in the executive protection program's objectives, the program is doomed to fail, because the principal doesn't like it and, in many cases, can change or end it in a moment's notice.

Executive protection managers must first understand the personal preferences of the principal, and then translate those into objectives that the team can work toward. Identifying and making these explicit is no easy task, but it is an essential one.

Key Takeaways	
All good executive protection programs must live up to four basic objectives:	
1	Match program deliveries to an ongoing analysis of the principal's profile and the resulting risks, threats, and vulnerabilities.
2	Conceive and implement the program according to best-practice executive protection standards.
3	Align the program with corporate or family objectives, practices, and culture.
4	Carry out the program according to the personal preferences of the principal.

Chapter 2-4:

This chapter takes a closer look at one of the key challenges of corporate or high-net-worth family executive protection: how to organize the team that will carry out the day-to-day protection of the principal.

Any executive protection program requires a certain set of competencies and will include roughly the same types of job descriptions. They do so differently, however, according to program comprehensiveness, complexity, maturity, and, of course, budget. Accordingly, all executive protection programs will require that the roles below be fulfilled in one way or another. Clearly, if one or just a few persons are responsible for covering all of the roles described below, such a program will have a very different level of effectiveness and quality than a more comprehensive one.

The most common executive protection program roles:

- Executive protection manager
- Executive protection agents
- Residential protection agents
- Covert protection agents
- Security drivers
- Protective intelligent agents
- Operations center agents
- Specialist executive protection partner

The Executive Protection Manager

The executive protection manager translates strategy into operations; leads and organizes the protection team; and acts as the bridge between the protection team, the principal, and the corporate or family office ecosystem. The manager is the one point of contact that all stakeholders look to — and hold responsible for — all aspects of the program.

Depending on the scope of the program, the role of executive protection manager can be filled in a variety of ways. But it should always be filled: it's essential that one person has overall responsibility for the program, and that this is clear to the chief security officer (CSO), the rest of the executive protection team, the principal, and other stakeholders throughout the corporation or family office.

Initially, a brand-new program might bring in a specialist partner on a consultant basis to act as a part-time program manager and help set up the program. This has the advantage of using a skilled practitioner who can draw on experience from other programs. Once the program is ready to be implemented, a solution that provides ongoing resources will be necessary.

Some programs might take another approach in their early stages and go the route of retaining one person with the dual role of local security driver and executive protection coordinator, but not manager. When this person isn't driving, they're able to work on other aspects of the program, such as liaising with a specialist partner to hire security drivers in other locations.

Once the decision to create a more comprehensive executive protection program has been made, the best way to begin organizing it is to assign it a manager. It will then be the manager's responsibility to ensure that the program is based on an up-to-date RTVA, write a suitable strategy, plan and organize program implementation, staff up, and ultimately run the program. Of course, all of this must be done with respect for the organization's culture and the principal's personal preferences, as well as in cooperation with the key corporate or family office stakeholders described above.

The manager can be either hired directly by the organization or "embedded" from a specialist partner. This second option has the advantage of placing the onus of recruiting and developing a new manager on an organization that has a proven track record and deep bench for doing just that — something few corporate and family office security or HR departments have any experience in.

The ideal executive protection manager will be a person with the right background and personality, who has come up through the ranks as a protection agent, and understands all practical aspects of the profession, and has experience in running programs in corporate and/or high-net-worth family settings.

Though not their specific role, the manager will often take a shift as a protection agent. While this might fill the occasional scheduling gap, the real reason for doing this is to stay close to the front lines to evaluate program and agent performance. The manager needs to discover and correct any issues that can affect program goals and coach agents accordingly.

At the same time, it's important the roles of manager and agent aren't conflated. If the manager falls into the trap of becoming the default, more or less permanent protection agent, then there will be no time to take care of managerial tasks. The manager who continues to act as an agent shirks the work of organizing, planning, and maintaining relations across the corporate ecosystem. The tough decisions about hiring, developing, and perhaps firing protection agents do not receive the attention they should. Not only does the manager-as-agent run the clear risk of jeopardizing program success — personal burnout is also all but guaranteed.

Executive Protection Agents

A cornerstone of every program, executive protection agents are responsible for providing close protection of the principal. And as we'll see in **Section 4: Managing Changes in Executive Protection Programs** those who are successful possess a unique mix of hard and soft skills and experience.

These are the persons who create and enforce the actual circle of protection around the principal as he or she moves throughout the day — whether at home, the office, or while traveling. They perform advance work when new locations need to be scouted and made safe. They're on the front line of ongoing security and productivity optimization for the principal, making sure logistics are as smooth as they can be and constantly adjusting plans and activities as needed.

I'm often asked how many executive protection agents are necessary to staff a program. Of course, the answer depends on the scope and nature of the program. In my experience, however, at least two full-time agents are needed to create the backbone of a good program, and this can be considered the minimum viable number of dedicated agents. This doesn't mean that two agents can provide full 24/7/365 coverage for any given principal. It does mean that a minimal team of an executive protection manager and two agents can provide excellent service (with the help of specialist partners as needed) and be a good foundation on which to build.

Such a two-person team is enough to provide solid coverage on a multi-country trip. The manager stays at home, and the two agents leapfrog between destinations. While the first agent is with the principal in one country, the second agent is in the next country doing advance work and double-checking necessary third-party resources such as security drivers, vehicles, or additional protective agents sourced through a specialist partner. This second agent stays in the country to welcome the principal and handle security while they're there; meanwhile, the first agent moves on to the next stop on the itinerary to do advance work there.

Executive protection agents can be either full-time employees of the corporation or family office or embedded from a specialist partner. Embedding agents from a partner has the advantage of trying out different agents to find those with the best fit with the organizational culture and principal. This can be a significant plus: despite all efforts to match the right people to the right jobs, the only way to really discover whether chemistry and personalities work well together in this people business is to try it out. If the principal's won organization has to recruit, hire, and fire to find the right people, this takes time and money that can be saved by drawing on a partner's deep bench.

Residential or "Fixed-Site" Agents

Depending on the nature of the threats to the principal and their family, residential security will often also be part of the security package.

Residential security is sometimes organized separately from corporate executive protection. However, there are good reasons to integrate the two efforts into one program. Such integration is much more likely to provide seamless coverage based on the same intelligence, managed by the same people, and according to the same principles.

While some practitioners maintain that the skills, person- ality traits, and experience requirements for residential agents are lower than those for executive protection agents, I don't believe this is the case. To my way of thinking, residential agents are simply executive protection agents who work at a fixed site rather than accompanying the principal between fixed sites and while traveling.

From a risk management point of view, most residences are, in fact, rather less secure than corporate campuses. There are far more home invasions than office invasions, and street crime is more of a worry for homeowners than for corporate offices. For one thing, access to corporate headquarters is typically much more restricted than access to homes due to perimeter barriers, security guards, integrated surveillance technology, biometric access control, and other features that many families wouldn't dream of for their homes. For another, the principal's time and place predictability is simply greater for primary residences than it is for the office. Figuring out where prominent people live is usually pretty straightforward.

One of the consequences of the COVID-19 pandemic is that many more people work remotely from home. This includes our principals, many of whom invite guests to meetings at their residences rather than to corporate headquarters. Thus, it's not unusual that a highly prominent principal receives highly prominent visitors at home.

It's also important to remember that residential agents often get tasked with jobs other than simply "guarding a house." They interact regularly with family members, guests, and tradespeople. They handle deliveries. They are likely the very first responders to medical emergencies or fires. And they frequently double as security drivers to bring children to school and other activities.

Those who still think of residential agents as "the B team" would do well to examine the actual threats and vulnerabilities related to residential security and to consider all 10 protective capabilities outlined in **Section 1: Necessity, Nature, and Scope of Executive Protection Programs**. Which skills, precisely, would a residential agent not need?

Covert Protection Agents

Covert protection programs integrate a combination of skills, tactics, and techniques used in executive protection, surveillance detection, and counter surveillance. The cumulative results are an effective form of protection without the appearance of overt security. While noticeable protection might be relevant and appropriate in some circumstances, it's not always that attractive for persons or families who need protection day in and day out.

Covert protection endeavors to ensure that threats and disturbances are kept as far away from the principal as possible — ideally without the principal ever having noticed them — and that they're dealt with as necessary, without drama or commotion. It adds a security layer that can be enhanced according to evolving risk factors.

By embodying a proactive approach, covert protection can scale to respond to changing needs. By maintaining a discreet protective perimeter around the principal, covert agents continually assess and evaluate current risks and threats vis-à-vis client security. Prevention is preferred to cure, and proactive procedures are always prioritized over reactive measures. This means that the principal can relax and feel safe. Should conditions require the team to scale up in order to mitigate risk, the principal need not notice.

Security Drivers

Like residential agents, security drivers may or may not be integrated members of the permanent executive protection team.

When the program requires frequent use of a trained driver in the same location, for example, to handle commutes between the principal's primary residence and workplace, then it often makes good organizational, protective, and economic sense to retain a dedicated person for this job. Conversely, as pointed out above, it would make no sense to hire a driver in locations that the principal visits only occasionally.

Protective Intelligence Agents

Executive protective programs depend on a steady flow of relevant, updated intelligence regarding evolving threats. Protective intelligence agents are the ones who keep this information fresh and flowing to the rest of the program.

Unfortunately, some practitioners still perceive RTVAs as a one-and-done deal. However, an outdated, stale RTVA can be worse than no RTVA. Basing current protection on old intelligence can easily give a false impression that the team is shaping its protective efforts according to a true picture of the principal's actual prominence and its resultant risks, when in fact it isn't.

The protective intelligence agent is charged with ongoing updates of the RTVA, which is critical to staying on top of the changing risk and threat scenarios that impact the principal. In addition to these updates, the intelligence agent will among other things also be tasked with monitoring social media, keeping an eye on POIs, staying up to date on news about the principal that may affect prominence and/or threat levels, preparing regular reports on other security-related issues important to the organization, and with writing ad hoc reports for destinations on the principal's itinerary.

The intelligence agent may be hired directly by the organization or embedded. Embedding the agent from a specialist partner lets them draw on the partner's entire worldwide network as well as on the organization's own resources.

Using Specialist Partners as Part of the Protection Team

The role of specialist executive protection partner is on this must-have role list for a reason: Unless you're planning for operations on the scale of the US president's Secret Service, it's simply not feasible to insource all aspects of a modern executive protection program.

This is most readily apparent with something like security drivers. While it might make good sense to hire a full-time security driver based at corporate headquarters, for example, it would be neither efficient nor safe for a corporate program to bring drivers from the United States to India for a short business trip. Local road conditions and traffic cultures are radically different, and a US driver couldn't be expected to acquire the linguistic, cultural, navigational, or driving skills necessary to do the job properly for a three-day, two-country visit. What does make sense is using a specialist partner who can arrange for vetted security drivers who live up to the same high standards as those applied at home. A reliable specialist partner with global reach can be expected to coordinate these and other services.

Drawing on specialist partners is a reliable way to respond quickly to changing circumstances — which may well be the one constant of a busy executive protection program. If the principal's threat level suddenly increases, specialist partners can be drawn upon to fill the agent gap until a more permanent solution is found or until the threat subsides. Similarly, specialist partners with well-established international networks can allow the program to scale flexibly, globally, and quickly, without adding headcount.

No Program Success without Sufficient Headcount

One of the easiest organizational traps to fall into, especially for new or growing programs, is insufficient staffing.

Once the manager has found and developed a handful of good agents, it can be tempting to rely on the same small cadre — even though these turn into 80-hour workweeks for the people involved. And although agents who thrive are resilient, resourceful, and self-motivated, even super agents can become overworked. This reduces their operational readiness, of course, but it harms the program in other ways, too.

In the short- and mid-terms, relying heavily on just a few people increases the likelihood of favoritism between the principal, manager, and agents. It's one thing to make sure the program respects the principal's personal preferences — also as regards the kind of agent that provides protection — but it's another thing altogether to think that only a few individuals can fill this role. Unless the team develops sufficient depth, it's doomed to fail.

In the longer term, of course, this kind of work-life balance is intolerable. Even the best and most dedicated of agents will find someplace else to work.

> To ensure program success, it's critical that programs are staffed realistically.

Why a One-Person Executive Protection "Team" Always Adds up to Trouble

Some potential clients believe an executive protection program with one full-time agent is a perfectly viable option. Sometimes, this is driven by a wish to sample a new and unfamiliar service in a way that's less committing than going all in. Other times, it might be an attempt to save money.

Realistically, however, a one-person executive protection "team" is an oxymoron at best. At worst, it's an accident waiting to happen. Inherently unsustainable for tactical, HR, and work-life balance reasons, such one-person shows never work for long. Either the principal loses confidence in the one person in whom confidence is essential, the super-agent, or the overworked agent realizes that their superpowers only go so far, for so long, before burnout becomes inevitable.

Do the math: It takes a minimum of three executive protection agents to provide full-time coverage for one principal

The average CEO works 63 hours per week. Yes, that's a lot of hours. But if that principal is to get full-time protective coverage during a five-day work week, then agents would need to work at least 73 hours per week.

Why? Because, in order to give principals the flexibility they require and allow some time for necessary planning and reporting, executive protection agents need to start the job an hour before the principal starts their day and keep working for an hour after the principal calls it a day. In fact, many programs stipulate 16 hours of coverage per day, or 80 hours per five-day work week, to be sure the principal is covered at all times except the eight hours a day reserved for sleep.

We haven't even talked about agents' predictable time away from the job used for training or planned vacations, or less predictable things such as sick days and PTO for all the other events life throws at us. Assuming that agents work an average of 40 hours per week to keep overtime down and maintain a sustainable work-life balance, it's reasonable to calculate with three agents to provide full-time coverage for the average CEO.

. . . and that's before any travel

Travel requires agents to perform advances of all the places their principal is scheduled to visit on a trip. A good advance takes about one hour per venue. Of course, principals try to make the most of their time on the road and pack in as many meetings as possible, sometimes up to 10 separate venues on a busy day. Add hospitals, hotels, and FBOs to the list, and you can easily add another 12 hours of agent time for every travel day by the principal. Let's remember the time agents need to travel to each and every destination, too.

Many CEOs typically travel at least half the time, so depending on where and how often the principal travels, it might be necessary to add at least one more full-time agent to the team.

Readiness Matters

Agent readiness, a critical component of any protective program, depends on training, management, and physical and cognitive abilities. If agents consistently clock more than 70 hours per week, you can be sure that neither their bodies nor minds will be performing at the top of their game. Are these the people you want to protect your principal? We think not.

Properly staffed protection programs provide time for regular physical fitness training and consistent sustainment training to keep perishable skills sharp. But they also enable a healthy work-life balance.

Overwork and work-related stress impact agent readiness in the short-, medium-, and long-term. And, yes, this can happen to even to toughest alpha types. Too much time on the clock and on the road leads to burnout. Too much time away from home easily results in unhappy relationships with significant others. These are massive distractions for anyone, including the people chosen to provide personal protection.

	Key Takeaways
1	It takes a minimum of three executive protection agents to provide full-time coverage for one principal.
2	**Key roles** • Executive protection manager • Executive protection agents • Residential protection agents • Covert protection agents • Security drivers • Protective intelligent agents • Operations center agents • Specialist executive protection partner
3	Proper staffing includes a healthy work-life balance to maintain agent readiness.

Chapter 2-5:

Motivating and communicating with the executive protection team

Everybody knows that communication is the lifeblood of the organization and one of the manager's most essential tasks. In fact, managers typically spend far more time communicating than on other managerial tasks such as setting objectives, organizing, following up on delegated tasks, and developing people.

If you think about it, the reasons for this are obvious. Without communicating program objectives clearly and consistently, the team won't know about them. Plans are meaningless when they stay in the manager's head. KPIs and corrective action instructions are worthless unless they're communicated, discussed, and, finally, understood and internalized.

And yet survey after survey reveals the most common employee complaint about management, across many types of organizations, is poor communication.

Although I don't have statistics on the state of communication in the executive protection industry, I'm quite sure they'd reveal a similar tendency. On the list of what makes or breaks good executive protection programs, effective communication will always be at the top.

It's especially important in the EP industry. Given the criticality of what we do, protecting the well-being and productivity of our principals, the importance of good communication in executive protection is only greater.

When communication breaks down — within the team, between the team and the principal, or between the team and other key stakeholders in the corporate or high-net-worth family ecosystem — program failure is just around the corner.

And when executive protection programs fail, the principal's security and efficiency are the first victims. The executive protection manager's job security could be the next.

Overcoming Communication Challenges in Executive Protection

Executive protection managers face a number of particular communication challenges; it's important they — as well as everyone else involved including team members, principals, executive administrative assistants, and others in the organizational ecosystem — be aware of them.

One set of challenges arises because the stakeholders with whom we communicate are many and varied. One day the manager may have to hammer through budget revisions in corporate finance; the next day they could be selecting agents to protect the principal's preschool daughter or giving feedback on a security driver in Nepal. Regardless, positive outcomes of all three examples depend heavily on good communication by the executive protection manager.

Another challenge occurs because team members are often scattered across time zones, and scheduling constraints can make it difficult to gather everyone in the same place. Especially in complex, 24/7/365 programs, some team members will always be on the road, at a residence, or handling a detail somewhere else. They won't be in the same room, yet they need to be on the same page regarding a wide variety of issues.

But the biggest challenge is probably because individual characteristics play such an important role in our field. Compared to many other endeavors, the nature of our work puts a lot of focus on team members' personalities and people skills.

Whereas a prickly bookkeeper might go far in a family office, or an eccentric marketer could enjoy a solid career as long as their campaigns create results, executive protection agents whose temperaments strike the principal as odd will not be long in that position. Communicating directly and often about issues that are closely related to a colleague's psychological makeup is by no means easy, but it's always important in executive protection management.

The Hallmarks of Good Communication for Executive Protection Managers

Because of the special nature of what we do, executive protection managers need to take a special approach to communication. We outline below some key characteristics of good communication in executive protection programs that need constant managerial focus — and the understanding of all stakeholders.

360-degree

Executive protection managers need to ensure good relationships throughout the corporate ecosystem. This includes the principal and their executive administrative assistant, of course, but will likely also comprise many other corporate, family office, and residential staff. It also includes everyone on the protection team, no matter where or when they work.

Executive protection managers need to make 360-degree communication a priority. This means regular meetings, phone calls, and reports; it also means making the most of each and every touch point that presents itself, whether it's a quick conversation between details or popping into someone's office when the opportunity arises. Of course, some stakeholders should be prioritized. But it must also be a priority to make the rounds and stay in touch with all relevant parties.

Proactive

Executive protection managers cannot afford the luxury of waiting to see what happens and then coming up with a plan. They need to think ahead, look around the corner, and be prepared for a range of eventualities before they materialize. The same holds true in communication.

It helps the executive protection manager to think proactively in all things communicative. Through regular dialogue with the executive administrative assistant, for example, the manager is always keen to discover issues while they're still small and fixable.

- What happened this week?
- What's happening next week?
- Why?
- How are we doing?
- Is there anything we can do better?

We tell our managers we always want the executive administrative assistant's folder to be empty. This means they must tackle issues as soon as they arise and never let minor irritations build into major problems. This can only happen through proactive communication.

Immediately responsive

When an executive protection manager discovers something that needs attention, it's important to respond quickly. This is due not least to the criticality of what we as EPAs do: When the well-being of our principal is concerned, postponing communication to a more convenient or comfortable time is not an option. Agents need to act on available information now, not save it for a yearly performance review.

Responsiveness is also necessitated by the personal nature of what we do. If the principal signals dissatisfaction with a team member, for example, it's better to act now than later: a quick coaching session might nip the problem in the bud. And if a personnel issue has already grown beyond repair, then it's up to the manager to take decisive action, and quickly communicate this, even though the message isn't a pleasant one.

Direct

There can be no beating around the bush when it comes to management communication in executive protection programs. Goals and expectations need to be crystal clear to all involved. Changing SOPs must be expressed with absolute precision and without any ambiguity. The same holds true for explaining and clarifying the needs of the client to staff members.

Being brutally honest doesn't have to mean being brutal, however. While direct communication that protects program integrity always takes precedence above other matters, it does matter that the manager treats everyone with civility. It's possible to be both completely honest and direct in one's communication and to do so with respect and empathy. In fact, it's absolutely necessary to achieve a well-run protection program.

Continual

Managers who are good communicators never rest on their laurels and take a break from communicating. They treat communication as a constant priority. They include regular meetings or calls in their plans, and they always find ways to make the most of any opportunity to establish a stake-holder dialogue.

Across time and geographic barriers

Communicating with the entire executive protection team means being available when and where people work. If some team members work only the graveyard shift of a residential detail, then the manager needs to make the time — and the effort — to show up and talk to people even though it's late.

Everyone on the team needs to be acknowledged and to know they're an important part of the whole. They must know that they're connected to the mother ship even though they might not see it every day and that the manager is aware of and interested in individual performance and ready to provide support as needed.

If team members don't feel this close connection, then there's a real risk they won't be up to date on changes in SOPs or client requirements. The probability of them becoming complacent increases, and the likelihood of the manager discovering the resultant drop in team readiness decreases.

Key Takeaways

The characteristics of good communication for executive protection managers include:

1	Using a 360-degree approach to establish and maintain good communication with all relevant stakeholders
2	Proactively discovering issues that could turn into problems through regular dialogue with key stakeholders
3	Immediately responding to relevant issues
4	Communicating directly, especially about difficult issues
5	Continual, ongoing focus on good communication
6	Communicating with all team members, including those who work the late shifts and remotely

Chapter 2-6:

Measuring the performance of the corporate executive protection team

As any successful manager knows, what gets measured gets done. Executive protection is no different, and developing a strong set of key performance indicators (KPIs) is essential to program success.

KPIs help the executive protection manager and other stakeholders in several ways:

- ◎ **Focus:** Good KPIs keep the executive protection team focused on what matters. The emphasis should be on goals that are shared and important (i.e., the ones that define the contours of program success).

- ◎ **Diagnostics:** KPIs help management get a clear picture of what's working well and what needs improvement. For executive protection, where people are the program's most important asset, KPIs need to track both qualitative as well as quantitative aspects of team performance.

- ◎ **Accountability:** When it comes to security teams, there must be no doubt about who is responsible for what. KPIs enable team members to see how they contribute — and managers to understand who is or isn't performing to reach program goals.

- ◙ **Preemptive corrective action:** Ongoing evaluations allow executive protection managers to identify norms and outliers over time, so they can proactively respond to performance developments before trouble hits. This helps us to maintain our focus on proactive, preventive measures rather than relying only on reactivity.

- ◙ **Transparency:** Even in successful executive protection programs, it's not uncommon to be asked, "What do you guys actually do, anyway?" KPI reporting helps demonstrate that executive protection is more like a fire department than a police department. When we're not fighting fires, we're getting better at it by practicing.

KPIs are not the same as metrics. Metrics measure individual data points, whereas KPIs are sets of quantifiable metrics that enable the executive protection manager as well as principals and other stakeholders to evaluate performance against strategic and operational goals.

Best-Practice KPIs for Corporate Executive Protection

While the KPIs for individual executive protection programs will vary according to circumstances, best practice dictates they all share the same basic characteristics.

Aligned with program goals

KPIs should always help us understand program performance compared to program goals. While any individual KPI — or its underlying metrics — won't necessarily explain program success or failure, a good KPI report lets us understand whether the executive protection program is meeting its stated objectives — and to what extent.

Important

You don't need to measure everything, just the important things. But sometimes important KPIs are made up of multiple metrics, none of which seems too significant in and of itself. For example, knowing how many hours team members spend on travel might not appear that critical, but the data can enable decisions on hiring remote staff and reduce overall program costs — as well as improve readiness. Similarly, because it's vital to monitor risk factors that can affect the principal's safety, correlations that affect prominence — for example, increased media exposure through planned PR activities — may be meaningful, as are travel days in emerging markets.

Understandable

It might seem obvious, but I've seen enough examples to the contrary that I want to point out that KPIs must be understandable for all involved. Security professionals have a tendency to rely on jargon and acronyms that corporate stakeholders might find difficult to comprehend. Be sure to translate tactical speak into transparent KPIs.

Measurable

KPIs must, of course, be based on measurable data. In a people business like ours, however, we shouldn't shy away from personal evaluations that hard-nosed accountants might sneer at.

Consistent

Over time, KPI reports let us understand developments and trends that might otherwise be difficult to spot. To be sure we're comparing apples to apples, the underlying data should be collected and correlated in a consistent way.

Timely

Some things need to get evaluated sooner rather than later in order to provide value. For example, a KPI review after every detail lets us learn lessons that can be applied immediately.

Don't Forget to Keep Track of Team Morale and Cultural Fit

Executive protection is a team effort, so evaluating the executive protection team's cohesiveness and ability to work together is important. Here are some things to consider for ongoing evaluation.

Shared sense of purpose

The executive protection team and key stakeholders must clearly understand the risks and threats to principals — and the benefits of mitigating those risks in a way that enhances productivity. The executive protection team must be seen as a valuable partner in supporting the safety, satisfaction, and productivity of our principals.

Shared sense of team standards and approach

It's essential the team understands and uses transparent operational standards for everything from simple scheduling to crisis procedures.

Good relationships and communication

Frictionless interactions within the team and between the team and key stakeholders are essential to program success. Though not as simple to capture as other metrics, KPIs should nonetheless be developed in order to evaluate how executive protection team members cooperate with each other and relevant corporate departments and personnel.

Good program fit with the principal's personal preferences and corporate culture

When executive protection teams achieve excellence, their presence is effective but unobtrusive. They facilitate productivity and security without being asked to do so and often without being noticed; they never make the principal think twice or miss a beat, but rather adjust to the corporate culture and the principal's lifestyle. Measuring this isn't simple — but it is essential.

Excellent team morale and readiness

It's common — and potentially disastrous — for executive protection teams to grow complacent. If nothing happens to the principal, that can easily be confused with program success. That's why it's essential to develop KPIs that track team members' morale and operational readiness.

Potential KPI Areas for Executive Protection

There is no one-size-fits-all KPI list for executive protection. Your ideal set will depend on whether your program is in start-up, turnaround, or sustain mode as well as specific program objectives. Nonetheless, see below for a number of factors that will be relevant for many programs, and around which KPIs may be developed.

KPI Areas

Ongoing Risk Assessment

- Principal prominence
- Travel destination risks
- Intel including social media monitoring
- Persons of interest

Key Stakeholder Satisfaction

- Principal/traveler feedback
- Principal productivity
- Key partner feedback (executive admins, corporate security, estate management, etc.)
- Program/vendor management feedback
- Event manager feedback

Responsiveness

- Availability and appropriateness of executive protection resources
- Issues addressed thoroughly and quickly
- Short-notice request performance
- Responsiveness to identified issues

Quality of Services Provided

- Program management/organization
- Deliverables
- On-ground support (agents and transportation)
- Administrative activities

Team Workload

- Travel days
- Domestic trips
- International trips
- Comp time

Readiness

- Training
- Drills
- Fitness evaluation

Quality of Communications

- Appropriate
- Accurate
- Clear and concise

Operational Transparency

- Execution to expectations
- Clear understanding of executive protection program by key stakeholders

Financial Performance

- Budget expectations set and met — good financial stewardship
- Responsiveness to identified issues

Key Takeaways	
The characteristics of good communication for executive protection managers include:	
1	Developing a strong set of key performance indicators (KPIs) is essential to the success of executive protection programs. • Establishing and using good KPIs enables better focus, diagnostics, accountability, preemptive corrective action, and transparency. • Best-practice KPIs for executive protection are aligned with program goals, understandable to all, measurable either quantifiably or qualitatively, consistent over time, used in a timely way, and cover the most critical aspects of the program. • KPIs should also be established for team morale and cultural fit.
2	Specific KPIs should be developed for: • Ongoing risk assessment • Key stakeholder satisfaction • Team responsiveness • Quality of protective services provided • Team workload • Team readiness • Communications • Operational transparency • Financial performance

Chapter 2-7:

Connecting the dots between regulations, standards, policies, procedures, and their operational applications

As in any other business, executive protection efforts need to be managed in accordance with all applicable legislation or regulations. Solid standards must be defined and enforced. Finally, procedures based on firm policies — all consistent with standards and regulations — need to be put into place. All of this points to the need for effective governance of executive protection programs.

This chapter intends to present a framework that executive protection management — as well as corporate management and even the board of directors that oversee corporate and family office executive protection programs — can use to connect the many layers that add up to effective governance and enable effective reporting and follow-up.

Why Does Your Executive Protection Program Need Good Governance, and Who Needs to Be Involved?

Ultimate responsibility for the governance of corporate and/or family office executive protection lies with the respective boards of directors, whereas executive protection management can and should be held accountable for the policies and procedures that drive program deliverables.

Proper program governance answers a range of important questions that include:

- ◎ Why do we have a corporate executive protection program?
- ◎ Are the program's structure and its operations in line with applicable legislation and company policies?
- ◎ Who is responsible for what?
- ◎ Who needs to know what about program performance metrics?

When these questions can be answered clearly and directly by executive protection management, the C-suite, and the board, you're likely operating a well-governed executive protection program.

The **risk management stakeholder matrix** introduced in `Chapter 1-1` is helpful here, as it encourages managers to consider the roles of all stakeholders whose decisions can impact programs.

Executive Protection Legislation and Regulations: A Work In Progress

Although it's beyond the scope of *The Protective Circle* to provide an overview of all applicable legislation, to my knowledge there are no federal or state laws written directly to impact executive protection. With that said, there are a number of regulatory and other legal issues that, depending on the situation and location, can affect a corporate executive protection program and its governance.

Licensing

Some jurisdictions require executive protection providers to be licensed. Most don't. To be on the safe side, be sure that any individual or company involved in your executive protection program — be it a full-time employee or a third-party vendor

— lives up to any applicable licensing requirements. This can include the provision of bodyguard, residential security services, specialized driving skills, or the use of firearms.

Duty of care

This issue is often discussed in vague terms but rarely dealt with specifically — until it's too late. The corporation needs to be aware of how the provision of executive protection services can mitigate known risks, and thus protect the organization against negligence suits.

Liability insurance

All executive protection providers should be covered by suitable liability insurance, and those responsible for procurement should consider it their responsibility to make sure security providers have suitable coverage.

IRS regulations

In the United States, the IRS may consider some executive protection services to be a taxable fringe benefit unless certain conditions are met. Fortunately, these conditions are broadly consistent with what a professionally conducted RTVA would conclude as the basis for an executive protection program. For example, IRS regulation §1.132-5(m) stipulates that security-related transportation services aren't considered taxable income when they're rendered in connection with a bona fide security concern.

Setting Standards for Good Executive Protection

Since you won't be able to find a set of commonly agreed standards for good executive protection in any textbook, you'll have to make your own.

In my mind, standards are different from policies and procedures in several ways. They should be seen as guiding principles rather than specific rules. They're value-based and not necessarily defined by simple objective criteria. They have to do with ethics, conduct, and performance.

Standards are important because they set shared expectations for everyone involved in the corporate executive protection effort, including the principal and their organization as well as all staff and vendors involved in program deliverables. Standards are what allow us to benchmark, distinguish good performance from bad, and decide between right and wrong in case of disputes.

While every executive protection organization will ultimately have to set its own standards of excellence, refer to the 10 "Guiding Principles" on page 166.

Policies and Procedures Make It Operational

Once you've defined the standards against which you want to develop your executive protection program, it's time to set your sights on developing policies and procedures.

Policies are written documents that express how the executive protection organization will deal with all key issues that impact program deliverables and adherence to agreed standards. Procedures are the step-by-step instructions that dictate how some aspects of some policies are implemented; SOPs typically refer to critical procedures from which deviation is least tolerated.

Guiding Principles

1	**The principal is the priority** The principal's four security needs (physical, productive, reputational, and lifestyle) are the foundation of protection excellence. Enough said.
2	**Comprehensiveness** Using the Protective Circle as a guide, all protective programs should be as comprehensive as resources allow.
3	**Trust** The principal must be able to trust the executive protection team; furthermore, everyone on the team and in contact with it must be able to trust one another.
4	**Consistency** An executive protection program is as good as it is consistent. There should be one set of policies and procedures, not several. Everyone on the team should use the same approach for the principal, so there are no favorites.
5	**Resourcefulness** The program must be resourceful. Agents and managers should be proactive, think ahead, and be ready to improvise when necessary.
6	**Cultural and personal fit** Since executive protection agents are up close and personal with the principal and their staff, it's imperative we fit in. If no one in a corporate or high-net-worth family environment uses "sir" or ma'am," then we don't either. It's all about not making the principal miss a beat: we must live and breathe as if we're a part of the organizational culture — because we are.

7	**Calm sense of urgency** Everyone in the service industry knows that good service is always time-sensitive; in our field, acting quickly can be critical. Nonetheless, it's imperative that executive protection providers never create unnecessary nervousness and that they keep things under control even in the face of surprises.
8	**Attention to detail** Many of the little things we do can have major repercussions — both because of what we do and for whom we do it.
9	**Controlled empathy** We do everything we can to keep our principal happy and productive. But sometimes the principal's security takes precedence. We're prepared to act on this even when it's not the most popular thing to do.
10	**Collaboration** Relationships with others in the principal's organization affect the program's efficiency, and thus both the principal's experience and security. Executive protection agents and managers can rarely pull rank to do what they need to do within the organization, so they have to earn respect and cooperation rather than rely on authority.

Establishing clear policies for executive protection programs is helpful for many reasons.

These are some:

- Policies ensure compliance with any relevant regulations and are explicit interpretations of the program's agreed standards.
- They enable program-wide consistency, even in times of change, so decisions are made in a uniform way in the field and at home.
- They establish a clear understanding of roles, responsibilities, and accountability, and facilitate reliable performance assessment.

We believe all executive protection programs should have policies and procedures that govern the following areas:

- Policies that impact legal liabilities

    - Confidentiality
    - Use of force
    - Insurance
    - Contracts

- HR-related policies

    - Physical fitness
    - Training
    - Career development
    - Performance assessment
    - Substance abuse
    - Vetting and background checks
    - Remuneration, pension, benefits
    - Internet, email, social media

- Financial policies

    - Budget planning
    - Expense reporting

- ◎ Travel policies
- ◎ Detail policies
- ◎ Advance work
- ◎ Coverage of the principal

  - ▫ At home
  - ▫ At work
  - ▫ While commuting
  - ▫ While traveling

- ◎ Reporting policies

  - ▫ Key metrics and KPIs
  - ▫ Trip/detail reporting
  - ▫ Monthly/quarterly/yearly reporting and business reviews

- ◎ Vendor and procurement policies

  - ▫ Make/buy decisions
  - ▫ Vendor approval
  - ▫ Vetting and control

Best Practice: Use It or Lose It

Executive protection policies and procedures are only useful if they're prepared well and used consistently. Here are a few things I've learned along the way.

Ownership and approval

Be clear on who owns the policy and who needs to be involved in its approval. While executive protection policies are usually developed by the executive protection manager, the chief security officer (CSO) will certainly want to be involved in making sure they are in line with overall security policies. Similarly, it's natural to reach out to corporate HR, legal, finance, procurement, and other departments to ensure the executive protection policies comply with other organizational standards.

Communication and training

Everyone impacted by a policy should have easy access to it and the opportunity to learn everything relevant about it. Sounds obvious, but it isn't always. Also, it's often not enough that staff are simply exposed to written versions of a policy. Careful training procedures let employees test and improve their understanding of policies and procedures.

Review

All policies should be reviewed on a regular basis to determine compliance and relevance. If the level of compliance isn't acceptable, then there's something wrong with either team performance or the policy itself; in either case, management must do something. If the policy is never used or is deemed to no longer have relevance, then it should be deleted.

Key Takeaways	
1	Governance of executive protection programs should be on the radar of the boards of directors for both corporations and family offices.
2	Different jurisdictions deal differently with a range of critical issues relevant to executive protection. Such issues include duty of care, liability insurance, licensing, and taxation of provided services.
3	The lack of common standards for good executive protection means that it's up to individual programs to establish their own standards.
4	All executive protection programs should establish clear policies for a range of areas, including anything that impacts finances, HR issues, legal liabilities, reporting, travel, vendors and procurement, and working details.

Chapter 2-8:

How to write an executive protection strategy

So, you want to write an executive protection strategy, and you're looking for a template. Good luck. Because, unlike many other aspects of organizational life, executive protection often seems to be implemented without a strategy.

There just aren't many executive protection strategy documents lying around either in corporate headquarters or in executive protection companies. Blueprints that cover the strategy essentials are not available online. Why? This is due to two simple but interrelated factors:

- Most people who know a lot about corporate strategy don't know much about executive protection.
- Most people who know a lot about executive protection don't know much about corporate strategy.

An Executive Protection Strategy Template Is a Good Start

Just because there aren't many examples to build on doesn't mean that a strategic approach to executive protection isn't important. Ask any business manager, military officer, or coach: A simple strategy is better than none, and a little planning goes a long way in winning both the battle and the war.

In this chapter, I share a process for planning executive protection programs for corporate and high-net-worth clients. I'll be the first to admit it: This template is far from rocket science, and a lot of my friends with MBAs could certainly come up with more cutting-edge corporate strategy templates.

Asking and answering the right questions in an orderly sequence will help everyone involved — on both the principal's and the provider's side of the table — to create a planning process and document that will make a huge difference.

Here's a skeleton template for an executive protection strategy. I'll leave it up to you to put some meat on the bones, and to answer the questions in a way that aligns best practices in the corporate, family office, and executive protection worlds.

Introduction

Summary

Feel free to write this after the rest of the plan is written. And be aware that many people won't read much beyond this, so write it carefully.

Statement of purpose

In broad terms, what are your reasons for creating an executive protection strategy? Why will the world, or at least your organization, be a better place once you have written a water-tight strategy?

Background

- How do the values, history, and business objectives of the corporation or family office relate to the executive protection strategy?
- Are there any events, developments or other reasons that make the plan necessary now?

- ◎ Feel free to use the Protective Circle as you think through the principals' different security needs, the various contexts in which they require protection, and the types of threats and vulnerabilities that are most relevant, but also consider:

  - □ Business risks
  - □ Board mandates
  - □ Duty of care and corporate liability issues

Objectives

What are you trying to achieve? Try to be as specific and measurable as possible.

- ◎ What are the goals and **expected outcomes/ results** of the executive protection program?
- ◎ What would be the **key benefits of achieving those goals** — for the corporation and for the principal?
- ◎ Can you boil the program down to some **simple guiding principles** that are easy for everyone to understand and remember?

Key success factors

What elements of the program are critical in order for it to be successful? Think, *If we get these things right, we are on our way to a great program.* What are those things?

KPIs

What do you need to measure in order to know whether your executive protection program is on track? Consider "hard" factors like budget and schedules — as well as "soft" factors such as principal satisfaction.

Governance

Who makes decisions about corporate executive protection? Based on what criteria?

> The personal risk stakeholder matrix presented in Chapter 1-2 is helpful here.

Situation analysis

This is similar to the well-known SWOT analyses so familiar to the corporate world. In the executive protection industry, we call this an RTVA. The purpose of the SWOT and the RTVA exercises is similar: Know where you stand before you start planning how to move ahead.

- ◎ Are there **direct threats** and security risks to the corporation or principal?
- ◎ Are there **indirect threats**, e.g., security risks not directly targeting the organization or its principal(s) but present in regions where the company operates?
- ◎ What would be the **impact**, or loss, should these threats be realized?
- ◎ What is the status/evaluation of our current executive protection and security programs?
- ◎ How do we evaluate security vulnerabilities?
- ◎ How vulnerable are we to identified threats?

  - ▫ Evaluation of current and past executive protection efforts: What lessons have we learned?
  - ▫ What parts of the corporate or high-net-worth family ecosystems are relevant to the executive protection effort?

- What are the `principal's personal preferences` regarding executive protection and their lifestyle?
- `Gap analysis:` Where we are now compared to our goals?

Executive protection program design

WHO will be protected?

- ◎ List of principal(s), corporate position(s) (CEO, COO, etc.), and family members that are to be protected by the executive protection program.
- ◎ Are all persons to be provided the same level of protection? Why or why not?

WHEN will the principals be protected?

- ◎ 24/7/365?
- ◎ Only while traveling for the company? To all destinations or only some?
- ◎ In other circumstances?

WHERE will the principals be protected? To all destinations or only some?

- ◎ At home
- ◎ At work
- ◎ While commuting home/work
- ◎ While driving, walking, etc.
- ◎ At corporate or other events
- ◎ At other family members' activities
- ◎ While traveling

  - `Abroad:` high-, medium-, and low-risk territories
  - `Domestic`
  - `Business`
  - `Personal`

WHAT kinds and levels of protection are necessary? Consider all of the 10 protective capabilities described in the Protective Circle:

- Conflict management/CQB
- Security driving
- Medical/hygiene
- Cyber/digital
- Protective intelligence
- Advances and secure travel
- Protective detail management
- Security sweeps
- Security escorts
- Fixed-site protection

Executive Protection Teams and Organization

- Draw the **organigram** (organizational chart) that describes the executive protection organization and its lines to other parts of the principal's organization.
- What are the key job descriptions and qualifications?
- How does the executive protection team **interface** with the rest of the corporate organization?

  - Stakeholder analysis: Who else in the organization does the executive protection team need to work with? Why is this important?
  - What are the communication procedures between the executive protection organization and other corporate departments?

- Training

  - What are our training program and procedures?
  - Who should be trained or certified for what and to what level?

- Career planning

  - How do we help executive protection agents and managers continue to develop their capabilities and careers, so they stay with us rather than move on?
  - Alignment with corporate HR strategies and procedures?

- Program scoping

  - How do we scale up or down as needs change?
  - Which costs should be considered as fixed and which are variable?

Procurement strategy

Technology

- Which tech do we need?
- How do we buy it?
- Does it align with corporate procurement strategies?

Human Resources

- **Make/buy:** Do we insource, outsource, or embed key executive protection positions? Be sure to check out Chapter 1-6 to address this question.
- The executive protection manager
- Executive protection agents

- ◙ Residential agents
- ◙ Intel analysts
- ◙ How do we search, shortlist, and evaluate the executive protection companies we want to work with?
- ◙ Are our contract management and policies in order?

Program delivery and maintenance

- ◙ What are the **SOPs** for all key processes?
- ◙ How do we **assess security risks on an ongoing basis**? How often do we update RTVAs? Do we do it ourselves, or ask for third-party assistance?
- ◙ How do we continually improve the skills of our staff?

  - ▫ Training
  - ▫ Security exercises and drills: frequency, scope, post-drill evaluation, data collection, etc.

- ◙ How do we **inspect and assess the quality** of our own security measures?

  - ▫ Internal evaluation
  - ▫ External audits
  - ▫ Red teaming

Reporting and KPI measurement

- ◙ Which **KPIs** do we follow and measure program success against? Consider both the "hard" criteria such as the well-being of the principal, budget adherence, etc., as well as the "soft" criteria such as the principal's satisfaction and team motivation.

◎ Which **reports** do we create on a regular basis? What do they contain? Who writes them? Who reads them?

◎ Which ad hoc reports will be necessary, and when?

Budget

◎ What are program **setup costs**?

◎ What are ongoing program costs?

    □ Fixed

    □ Variable

◎ Who has budget responsibility?

◎ What are the procedures for financial reporting?

◎ What do we do about budget/actual deviations?

Implementation plan

◎ What are the critical path milestones for developing and implementing the executive protection program?

◎ Who has responsibility for moving the program forward?

◎ Who approves what, when?

Appendices and additional notes

◎ Is there extra information relevant to the strategy?

◎ Do we need a glossary of terms?

◎ References and resources

◎ Special circumstances

So, there you have it, a tried and tested way to structure an executive protection strategy. Time spent on developing such a strategy is well spent and even if you don't fill in all of the blanks, covering the main points will serve your program well.

	Key Takeaways
	Corporations and family offices that require executive protection should articulate strategies that include:
1	**Introduction** • Summary • Statement of purpose • Background • Objectives • Key success factors • KPIs • Governance
2	**Situation analysis** • RTVA • SWOT analysis
3	**Program design** • Who will be protected • Where and when they will receive protection • What kinds of protection they will receive • Which capabilities agents and managers must master to provide protection • How the team is organized
4	**Procurement** • What will be insourced • What will be outsourced
5	**Program delivery & maintenance** • SOPs • Ongoing RTVA updates • Training • Reporting and KPI measurement
6	**Budget**
7	**Implementation plan**

SECTION 3:

The Importance of Training

Programs without sustainment training are not sustainable.

Acme's path to a full-time protection program for its CEO was similar to many other corporations' before it. The tech company began by using different vendors — a local guard company for residential security, limo services for driving, and various ad hoc solutions for protection while traveling — but after the board mandated full-time protection for the principal in response to growing risk, the CSO and the principal decided they needed a different approach. So, the decision was made to set up a more comprehensive program, hire a full-time director to manage it, and issue an RFP to find one vendor that could handle it all.

To head up the new program, Acme's CSO first hired Frank. Working with procurement, Frank and the CSO embarked on a journey to find the perfect vendor for a program that included full-time residential security, security drivers, and travel protection for the CEO and certain members of her family. After meticulous rounds of requests for proposals (RFP) and arduous contract negotiations, they finally chose a vendor and commenced their new EP program.

The program flourished under Frank's watchful eye, and the vendor's team swiftly transitioned from nonexistence to an efficient force, leaving no room for doubt about their competence. Frank got plenty of kudos for his accomplishments, which did not go unnoticed in the relatively small world of corporate executive protection. In fact, Frank's stint at Acme didn't last long. After only 18 months, he was headhunted for a job with a bigger program, and Acme hired John to replace him.

One of John's first initiatives in his new role was to conduct a SWOT analysis of the program. Things were undoubtedly going well. The vendor was hitting its KPIs and the principal was pleased with the coverage. Naturally, both John and the CSO were keen to keep things moving in the right direction. During this evaluation, however, John discovered a critical oversight — the absence of sustainment training for the agents. Renewing certifications for vital first aid qualifications and maintaining other perishable skills, such as defensive and evasive driving tactics, had been "overlooked" during the previous procurement and contracting processes. And when sustainment training wasn't dealt with in the RFP, it was no wonder that wasn't included in the scope of work, either, or that no KPIs regarding it had been agreed upon.

At first glance, the lack of sustainment training seemed like a small issue. After all, the program was running smoothly, and the EP agents were performing their duties effectively. However, the revelation concerned John. How would the program thrive in the medium- and long-term without the training necessary to maintain agent skills? It was no use blaming Frank or the procurement team. Frank had moved on, and procurement had no way to understand the significance of such training. But the vendor, who had intimate knowledge of the industry, certainly understood the importance of sustainment training? After asking a few questions, John learned the vendor had felt forced to exclude sustainment training from the RFP to keep costs at a minimum. In the competitive realm of RFP responses, the vendor had learned the hard way about adding activities and costs not explicitly stated in the initial proposal.

John knew there was no simple fix to the problem. Finance had made clear that there could be absolutely no overspending on unbudgeted course expenses or for bringing in additional agents to cover while the FTEs trained. Beyond the issue of budget, however, there was also the challenge of operational continuity. Although perishable skills would soon become rusty without regular training, the agents were already overworked and even finding time for contracted PTO was difficult. So, squeezing multiple days of offsite training into overstretched working schedules wasn't feasible.

With the contract period set to expire soon anyway, John hoped that a new RFP round might solve the problem. Procurement was fine with that as long as the vendor, not Acme, would bear any additional training costs. After all, they argued, it was the vendor's employees that needed training, not Acme's. And since corporate guidelines clearly stipulated that vendor expenses were frozen for the next two years as part of a cost-cutting exercise, the same RFP was used again.

At John's encouragement, the incumbent vendor included redundancy in staffing costs to allow for regular training. They were transparent about the need for sustainment training and its related expenses and were in no doubt that Acme should pay for the costs of training agents who worked exclusively for Acme's own program. However, one of the two other companies that made it to the final round again cut sustainment training from their proposals to keep costs down. In the end, that company won the bid and replaced the incumbent vendor. History repeated itself, and the program continued without sustainment training. The highest-potential agents quietly packed their bags and found other jobs. Operational readiness began to degrade, and program quality began to suffer. Ultimately, John, too, left Acme — but not voluntarily.

Chapter 3-1:

As introduced in **Section 1: Necessity, Nature, and Scope of Executive Protection Programs**, the outermost ring of the Protective Circle consists of the 10 protective capabilities. This is the "how" of executive protection — the competencies that agents must master to mitigate risk. These personal competencies are a prerequisite of protective readiness, and program success depends on agents who master them to one extent or another.

Agents acquire these competencies through training, on-the-job experience, and mentorship. While all three are necessary and build upon each other, training plays a foundational role. Ideally, all agents should have basic training in these 10 protective capabilities to qualify them for their first job. Only then can they build their tradecraft as they solidify these competencies through experience and further hone them through mentorship. Unfortunately, however, training in executive protection is a little bit like flossing your teeth. If they think about it, everyone knows it's important and that they should do it regularly; still, many don't get around to it as often or as seriously as they should.

This section will focus on agent training — not the training of team leads, supervisors, or executive protection managers. The capabilities introduced and discussed below are relevant for all agents to provide good protective coverage. In addition to mastering these, those who aspire to management roles must also acquire a range of managerial competencies to successfully navigate the issues we described in **Section 2: Managing the Executive Protection Program**. Indeed, the lack of well-trained managers and dedicated management training courses is a problem for the industry and its growth prospects — but that's a separate problem.

Though *The Protective Circle* doesn't include exercises or physical requirements for EPAs, that doesn't mean that being in good physical shape is irrelevant to executive protection. On the contrary, it's highly relevant, and many programs require that agents be able to pass basic physical examinations on a regular basis.

Ten years ago, agent training was more of an afterthought than a priority — something that was nice to have if time allowed, but time was always tight. Five years ago, training was rarely mentioned in RFPs, but things are changing. Training, learning, and development are finally getting the attention they deserve in executive protection, especially in the larger programs, but the industry still has a long way to go.

The lack of standards is a significant challenge. Training requirements vary from country to country and between executive protection companies. There are no internationally agreed standards, and most countries have none at all. Executive protection schools all have their own takes on how much basic training in each of these disciplines is necessary and even if all 10 are necessary. Like everything else in *The Protective Circle*, these thoughts on training represent my views not those of the "aligned executive protection industry," whatever that is. While there are some who hold these views, there are many who don't.

This chapter aims to underscore the importance of training for program health and for the well-being of our principals and agents alike. There are at least 10 good reasons why training is so critical to the success of executive protection programs.

Training Is the Only Way to Acquire the 10 Basic Capabilities of Executive Protection

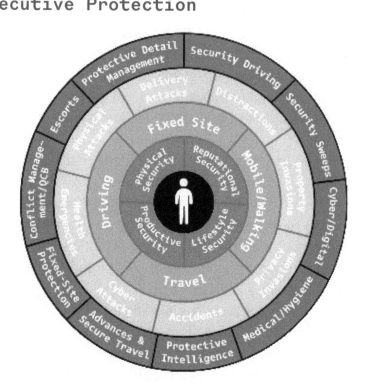

Each of these 10 basic capabilities is a combination of "hard" and "soft" skills. This chapter discusses the "hard" aspects, i.e., technical, physical, or methodological skills that must be mastered to achieve competency. People aren't born with these skills, so they must be acquired through effort. While they can be learned either formally or informally, we will first deal with formal learning — the organized, intentional kind that happens in classrooms, online, or in other dedicated learning environments, not the unstructured, spontaneous kind.

At least three of these capabilities are relevant in other contexts and can be acquired in other domains, such as the military or law enforcement. Broadly speaking, it's relatively straightforward to transfer these skill sets to executive protection.

These include:

- ◎ Conflict management/CQB
- ◎ Security driving
- ◎ Medical/hygiene

The remaining seven capabilities are more specific to executive protection. Though they can be learned in other contexts, they're typically acquired in dedicated executive protection schools or internal courses:

- ◎ Cyber/digital
- ◎ Protective intelligence
- ◎ Advances and secure travel
- ◎ Protective detail management
- ◎ Security sweeps
- ◎ Security escorts
- ◎ Fixed-site protection

Training Enables Agents to Acquire New Skills

Everything changes — including the skills executive agents need to acquire and master. No matter what agents learned once upon a time, including basic training in the 10 capabilities outlined above, they will likely need to add to those to adapt to changing protective demands.

Keeping up with the possibilities and vulnerabilities of new tech is one thing, but there could be many others. For example, if the principal adds a baby to the family, agents might be asked to learn about pediatric first aid and the proper installation of car seats. If a pandemic changes the way people live and work, agents might need to add a variety of new skills to their repertoire — anything including enhanced hygiene procedures or residential mail screening that may accompany their working at home. Furthermore, as the executive protection industry professionalizes, new training is essential to keep up with the latest trends and best practices.

Training Keeps Perishable Skills Fresh: Use It or Lose It

As explained further in **Chapter 3-5**, sustainment training is essential to keep certain capabilities up-to-date and usable. These comprise conflict management/CQB — including the use of firearms when relevant, security driving, and medical/hygiene. Depending on the nature of the program, others might be relevant.

Fortunately, agents rarely if ever need to call on skills such as operating a heart defibrillator or engaging in evasive driving. However, this doesn't mean these skills are unimportant or irrelevant. Executive protection managers and HR departments need to realize that these are all perishable skills. If agents don't use them, they lose them — and might not be able to apply them when required.

Regular sustainment training schedules need to be developed for all teams and all agents. Some of this training will be off-site at dedicated facilities and with specialized instructors. Some of it will take place around a conference table at departmental meetings and be conducted by the manager or a team member with subject matter expertise. Some skills can be learned and maintained via online training as well. All of it is important.

More than once, I've run into corporate HR departments who roll their eyes at EP requirements to keep something as essential as security driving skills up to date. Didn't the agent just do that 18 months ago? Isn't zipping around a racetrack at high speed more fun than necessary? When has anything ever happened while the principal was being driven around town?

These are all reasonable questions for people with no experience in executive protection. In these cases, and many others, the manager needs to step up and explain the importance of ongoing training both to meet the program's goals of protecting the principal and to develop and retain the best talent to do it.

Training Helps Personalize Protective Programs

All clients are different, and no two executive protection programs should be identical. Therefore, training can be an essential way to enable agents to deliver the kind of personalized protection that our clients increasingly expect.

Training Keeps Standard Operating and Emergency Procedures Sharp

Having SOPs for everything is great, but if they're in a binder that no one ever sees and never get trained, they really aren't of much practical use.

Training is the bridge that connects ideas on paper to action in the field. It enables new agents to learn "how things are done around here," and it helps established teams keep critical but seldom-used emergency procedures fresh and reliable. And training is a much better way than operational drops to allow managers to discover just how "standard" SOPs actually are, and whether agreed ways of dealing with emergencies work when the pressure is on.

Training Management Is an Essential Component of Quality Management

The quality of any protective program depends on the capabilities and engagement of the people providing it. Similarly, the fact that training is key to capability development and motivation should surprise no one. It would follow logically, then, that training management is crucial to overall quality management. However, this simple fact is too often overlooked in executive protection.

Training management goes hand in hand with quality management. The KPIs that delineate quality must be clear, and training must enable agents and managers not only to achieve the prescribed quality, but also to distinguish acceptable quality from the unacceptable. Systematizing the integration of training and quality management has great potential to improve both.

Training Combats Complacency

Fortunately, emergencies are a rare occurrence for most protective teams. After all, most of the time the principal's life and well-being are not immediately threatened.

What's not so rare is complacency: When nothing extraordinary usually occurs, it's easy for teams to think they're prepared even if they're not. The difference between a complacent and a ready team can be impossible to discern for the clients. Unfortunately, many practitioners also fail to withstand complacency's almost gravitational pull. Keeping seldom-used skills sharp just in case anything bad happens is much more difficult than letting them slide.

Regular training keeps complacency at bay by forcing teams to stay on their toes, even when no one's watching.

Training Improves Compliance and Reduces Liability in Executive Protection Programs

The legislation, regulations, and organizational norms with which executive protection teams must comply vary greatly by context. Laws specific to personal protection, if they exist at all, are different country by country and state by state. Corporations and family offices all have their own general guidelines and governance procedures that may be applicable to protective situations and personnel. Even insurance policies, coverage, and fine print can vary widely. The same goes for contracts between clients and providers: in some cases, compliance issues will be included in RFPs and specified in scopes of work. Alas, often, they're not.

Regardless of the complexity, compliance with the letter and spirit of many possible stipulations is essential to protect our principals, their organizations, our agents, and our own companies — not from perpetrators, but from litigation.

Training is thus an essential way to reduce liability, and not only in litigious countries like the United States. Whether the subject matter is rules for the use of force, labor laws, local or international traffic regulations, or a myriad of other topics, training is crucial to ensure compliance and legal protection for our clients and ourselves.

Training Is Key to Attract, Develop, and Retain Executive Protection Talent

Finding good executive protection talent is already difficult in many circumstances and will only get harder. Of course, training is always necessary to develop talent, but when the industry is growing faster than the talent pool, training is also an important way to attract and retain it.

We know from recruitment processes that the availability of training matters greatly to quality candidates. They believe, correctly, that training is a reliable indicator of an employer's professionalism and willingness to help employees build careers. When demand for good agents is greater than supply, the best agents will look at a job's training opportunities and include these in their decision-making.

We also know from exit interviews that the lack of training opportunities is often cited as a reason to quit. Career development planning has been a staple of other corporate departments for decades. Now, security and HR directors are finally waking up to the fact that executive protection programs also rely on professionals who pursue career opportunities — if not here, then somewhere else where training and other career opportunities are more readily available.

Training Is an Investment, Not Just an Expense

Training costs both money and time. Tuition and travel costs are relatively simple to budget, but unless the time necessary for training is built into staffing levels, finding or making time for training in rotational schedules can be an even greater challenge for many programs.

Managers responsible for executive protection need to understand not only the direct costs of training but also the opportunity costs of not providing their staff with quality training. Yes, training requires resources, but so does backfilling open positions and replacing agents who have moved on to greener pastures. Regular investment in training pays big dividends.

If Training Is So Important, Then Why Doesn't It Happen as Much as It Should?

I hope you've been convinced of the importance of training for good executive protection. And you might be wondering, why does the author keep harping on this? It's because good training is unfortunately not nearly as common as it should be. At first glance, the main reason for this unfortunate situation is budgets and the competitive bidding process. Dig deeper, and you'll see that operational continuity also plays a related and quite significant role.

Training is rarely emphasized enough in RFPs and SOWs. If mentioned at all, it's rarely an integral part of the proposal or a parameter against which competing offers are compared. To really think training into a program, we need to budget both the actual out-of-pocket costs and the staff redundancy required to maintain operational continuity: When one agent is training, another needs to cover that shift, which requires staff redundancy — not a winner when bids are compared on price. This is gradually changing and is much better than it was some years ago, but the EP industry still has a long way to go before training gets the attention it should.

This becomes even more clear once programs get started. Even when the client organization understands the importance of training and is willing to pay for it, the principal's need for coverage always has a higher priority than agent training. No executive protection company is going to say, "Sorry, we can't help the principal with that trip — several of our guys have booked training on those days."

Key Takeaways

The protective capabilities required to keep principals safe and productive all require agents with proper training. there are at least 10 good reasons why training is critical to program success:

1	Training is the only way to acquire the 10 basic capabilities of executive protection.
2	Training enables agents to acquire new skills.
3	Training keeps perishable skills fresh: Use it or lose it.
4	Training helps personalize protective programs.
5	Training keeps standard operating and emergency procedures sharp.
6	Training management is an essential component of quality management.
7	Training combats complacency.
8	Training improves compliance and reduces liability in executive protection programs.
9	Training is key to attract, develop, and retain executive protection talent.
10	Training is an investment, not just an expense.

Chapter 3-2:

Separating the hard and soft skills of executive protection – and introducing tradecraft

There are plenty of discussions these days about hard and soft skills in executive protection, and that's a good thing. However, much of this talk is ambiguous at best and downright confusing at worst. Admittedly, I'm probably responsible for at least some of this muddle because I've been talking about hard and soft skills for years without always providing a clear definition of what's what, why each matters, and how to develop both. This chapter will help clarify things.

What's So Hard about Hard and Soft Skills?

Distinguishing between hard and soft skills is common in many industries, not just executive protection. Hard and soft skills are on the agenda of every HR director, and recruitment platforms such as LinkedIn and Indeed have spent plenty of time on the subject. Here, I want to clarify how the concepts of hard and soft skills are generally understood, and why I think these make good sense for executive protection, too.

Hard skills

Hard skills are akin to technical competencies. Accountants need to learn about general accounting principles and related legislation. Architects must be able to perform structural calculations and use AutoCAD. Such skills are called "hard" because they are less squishy than soft skills, not because they are difficult to learn — although they might be.

Hard skills are usually specific to a professional domain and are not something the rest of us pick up in grade school or high school.

Hard skills are typically measurable — things you can test. Indeed, many professions and industries develop evaluation and certification schemes to measure how well people master these skills — and whether or not they can hang out their shingle as, for example, an accountant or architect.

People typically learn hard skills through education, training, and experience.

Soft skills

Soft skills are more like personality traits than hardcore technical know-how. They refer to interpersonal and intrapersonal abilities such as emotional intelligence, problem solving, and communication, which are important in social environments that require collaboration. Soft skills are all about how we work with others and on our own. This is the squishy stuff, but that doesn't mean it's unimportant — quite the opposite.

Soft skills are more universal than specific, and they are transferrable and useful across most any profession. Everything else being equal, accounting firms want to hire candidates who demonstrate excellent soft skills, just like architectural practices, software startups, and McDonald's. However, just like hard skills, the variety of soft skills matters differently in different professions.

Soft skills are harder to measure in simple tests than hard skills, but they can be evaluated. Personality and other tests predict competencies in soft skills with some success, but the real proof is in the pudding: It's when we work with people over time that we get a good idea of their soft skills and how these skills, or lack thereof, affect work performance.

To some extent, soft skills depend on choosing the right parents. Some folks are just easier to be around and cooperate with than others. But with effort (sometimes a lot of it), anyone can develop their soft skills to at least some extent. Importantly, even small improvements can make a huge difference. Training can help.

Generally speaking, most people can learn the hard skills of executive protection fairly easily and apply them in a job. To keep the job, however, they need to master soft skills. In fact, insufficient soft skills are the most common reason agents get fired.

Both Hard and Soft Skills Matter in Executive Protection – So Does Tradecraft

As we'll see below in **Chapter 3-3** and **Chapter 3-4**, executive protection agents need to learn a variety of hard skills within each of the 10 protective capabilities. They must also apply some soft skills in conjunction with each. They also need something we call "tradecraft."

Strictly speaking, tradecraft refers to the techniques and procedures of espionage and intelligence gathering. Within executive protection, we define it differently. For EPAs, tradecraft refers to the enhancement of protective capabilities that come through experience, but experience on its own isn't enough. Tradecraft also requires mentorship. It's social learning, the kind we do by observing and imitating others as we work together. Tradecraft can at one level be considered the bridge between hard and soft skills: You need proficiency in both before tradecraft becomes relevant. We learn tradecraft on the job, sometimes the hard way. Hopefully, more experienced colleagues with a well-developed sense of tradecraft will make things easier.

Members of isolated teams sometimes have trouble developing their tradecraft. They might master the hard skills and demonstrate excellent soft skills, but because their opportunities for social learning are limited, they tend to repeat themselves and not grow and learn as much as they would in other settings.

To illustrate how these things work together, let's look at security escorts, one of the basic protective capabilities utilized in mobile/walking security contexts.

Standard executive protection training always includes an introduction to a variety of escort formations, e.g., the "diamond," and when to use them. These are hard skills. The ability to set up and carry out the diamond formation is a technical competency that's specific to the domain of executive protection. The skill can be acquired on or offline, but it needs to be learned. Proficiency in its execution is measurable: We can develop simple tests to evaluate how well agents have understood when and where the diamond formation should be used and how to set it up. Technically speaking, after some training and a little test, the agent has gained competency in this escort formation and is ready to go, right? Wrong.

Without empathy and other soft skills, agents that play by the book and simply apply the diamond formation as taught probably won't last long. Although the diamond might be completely appropriate in a given situation from a risk mitigation point of view, if it bothers the principal for whatever reason (e.g., they don't want to look like someone who needs the protection of several agents to get from a car to a building), it's probably better to find another way to provide mobile/walking protection. This is where tradecraft comes in.

Agents with experience have likely been in this situation before. If they're lucky, they've worked with seasoned managers and other agents who have shared their understanding of best practices when the diamond is indicated but practically impossible because it's bothering the principal. As an example, I can sum it up like this:

- **Hard skill:** Knowing when and how to set up the diamond protective formation
- **Soft skill:** Using social skills to understand how the diamond is affecting the principal's psychological well-being
- **Tradecraft:** Improvising a protective formation less stringent than the diamond — or coming up with a completely different solution — to keep the principal safe and happy (or at least happy enough)

How Good Managers Help Build Tradecraft

Executive protection managers are instrumental in enabling both the formalized training and the informal learning that equips staff to grow. If they aren't living and breathing this responsibility every day, then they aren't doing their jobs.

Good managers seize every chance to create learning and development opportunities. Instead of saving everything for a yearly review, they'll make use of even a little downtime to learn more about their staff's developmental interests and career goals.

Once a detail is completed and it's time for an after-action review, they'll ask simple questions like, "What are the lessons learned?" When they plan a new detail they'll consider (and inquire into) how individual agents can contribute and what they'd like to learn. What would it take to bump the person up a notch in terms of responsibility?

The learning-oriented manager always makes it a point to keep everyone on the team informed of the big picture. What's going on in the organization that can impact our work? Where are the best practices that can inspire us to do better? How are others embodying the values that we want to inform our work?

As executive protection managers, we need to take learning and development seriously. Think back on the teachers you had while growing up, and you'll probably remember one or two with particular fondness. Do the same with the list of managers you've had throughout your career: some will stand out as people who have been instrumental in helping you make career progress. We've all met them. We need more of them in the executive protection industry.

Key Takeaways
Hard skills, soft skills, and tradecraft are all important to develop good executive protection agents

1	**Hard skills** • Similar to technical competencies • Domain specific • Measurable • Learned through education, training, and experience
2	**Soft skills** • Similar to personality traits • More universal than domain specific • Harder to measure than hard skills, but can be evaluated • More inherited than learned and not as easy to acquire or improve as hard skills, but training can help and make a huge difference
3	**Tradecraft** This is a critical part of the executive protection capabilities package that's developed via experience and mentorship. Good managers prioritize building tradecraft whenever they can.

Chapter 3-3:

Training and the 10 protective capabilities

This chapter provides an overview of the training necessary for the 10 protective capabilities in Ring 4 of the Protective Circle. Before we get there, however, I'd like to emphasize a few things.

First, I'd like to ask those who equate executive protection with security guarding to think again: The kinds and degrees of competency required to work in executive protection far exceed those necessary in the rest of the security industry. Candidates need dedicated executive protection training and real-life security experience just to get in the door and will need more training and certifications to move up.

Also, it's important to note that most of the capabilities described below involve specialist skills unique to the executive protection industry. With the exception of conflict management/ CQB, medical/hygiene, and security driving (which are, generally speaking, largely transferable from other domains), the skills required for executive protection are different than those developed in law enforcement, the military, or other security-related fields. Indeed, we usually recommend that even highly qualified vets and ex-police officers take dedicated executive protection training before looking for work as agents. For one thing, the actual skills used are often different. For another — and, perhaps, even more importantly — the contexts in which they're used and the power relationships involved are also quite different. Soldiers and police are used to working in hierarchical organizations and often have a monopoly on the legal use of force. People follow their orders because they have to. Executive protection agencies often work in situations where authority is established not so much by their place in a hierarchy but by their creativity, resourcefulness, and, sometimes, their chutzpa. People follow their requests because they want to.

Let's also remember that, like the entire industry, executive protection training is not a tightly regulated or standardized affair. The good schools are run by professionals who have real-life executive protection experience and are also great teachers. The not-so-good schools are also trying to make a buck. It can be hard for clients, newcomers, and even experienced agents to know how to know what training is necessary, and where the best trainers do their teaching.

Finally, it's critical to note that the training people actually get varies according to risk scenarios, program complexity, and, yes, budgets. In many programs, a few agents may be responsible for all aspects of the Protective Circle. Ideally, these agents will have at least basic training in all 10 capabilities outlined below. This is, unfortunately, not the case. In more complex, professionally run, and well-funded programs, a larger group of agents will be responsible; all will have good basic training; and some will have more expertise in specific domains than others.

A Quick Overview of the 10 Protective Capabilities

Protective Capabilities Training	
Protective Intelligence	
Purpose	Understanding the changing nature of the principal's personal risk
Basic training	This skill set is underprioritized in many basic executive protection training courses, but good courses are available. The basics include learning how to RTVAs; fundamentals of info gathering and analysis; understanding and dealing with persons of interest (POIs) and groups of interest (GOIs) and persons to be on the lookout for (BOLOs).
Advanced training	Depending on program needs, further training might be relevant within many other areas, for example, internet/social media research methods, managing and working with GSOCs, and travel intelligence and location-based risk analysis.
Necessary sustainment training	Sustainment training isn't common in most programs.
Fixed-Site Protection	
Purpose	Protecting the principal at known, given locations

Basic training	Providing protection in sites like corporate offices and campuses, residences, hotels, conference centers, and event venues; safeguarding against property and privacy invasions, fires, and natural disasters; understanding protective security rings, e.g., perimeters, shells, cells, and using a layered approach; working with and without CCTV, sensors, alarms, etc.
Advanced training	There are many advanced training opportunities in all of the above, for example, procedures for working halls and walls, mail and packaging screening, or event security.
Necessary sustainment training	Sustainment training isn't common in most programs.
Advances and Secure Travel	
Purpose	Preparing and supporting the principal's trips to new, lesser-known locations to maximize security and productivity while there
Basic training	Training in advances and secure travel should be part of any basic executive protection course curriculum. However, before learners train in advances, they should have a solid understanding of how good protective operations work so they can then plan how these are best applied in a new location. Basic advance training will typically include segments on pre-advances and location desk research as well as on-site advances and advance reports.

Advanced training	Advanced training opportunities for advances are limited, but I've seen courses that cover: multi-location trips and trips that include multiple persons in the principal's party; how to leverage advance reports to improve customer relations and budgeting; and developing and reusing SOPs for things like halls and walls.
Necessary sustainment training	While not training per se, update SOPs and checklists with a critical eye at least annually.
Security Driving	
Purpose	Traffic accidents are a significant risk for everyone on the road, and secure driving skills to keep the principal safe in vehicular travel are among the most used of all executive protection skills.
Basic training	Many courses cover vehicle dynamics, defensive/evasive driving, protective driving, offensive driving, and vehicle inspection/maintenance are available; courses on client services and interaction are much more limited.
Advanced training	Depending on needs, a variety of more advanced courses are available, including counter ambush, ramming and pit maneuvers, winter driving, vehicle sweeps, driving with children, and front right.
Necessary sustainment training	Repeat basic training at minimum every two years, preferably annually or semi-annually.

Mobile/Walking Security	
Purpose	Getting the principal from A to B on foot securely
Basic training	Escorts, arrivals and departures, walking formations and routes
Advanced training	Covert protection
Necessary sustainment training	Sustainment training isn't common in most programs.
Medical/Hygiene	
Purpose	Keeping the principal healthy and, if necessary, alive until emergency room or other care can be provided
Basic training	Executive protection professionals must be trained in first aid/emergency medical procedures at the healthcare-provider level, including CPR and AED use. As we learned during the COVID-19 pandemic, they must also receive training in preventive hygiene procedures.
Advanced training	Depending on program needs, many types of advanced training might be relevant, for example, pediatric first aid, wilderness first aid, medical advances, or medical team management.
Necessary sustainment training	Repeat basic training annually.

Conflict Management/CQB	
Purpose	Protecting the principal from threats at close quarters
Basic training	**Conflict management** Techniques for diagnosing, preventing, and resolving conflicts — of the three skill areas mentioned here, this is certainly the one that is most often used. **CQB** We refer here only to unarmed CQB, where physical force is required for protection. Many agents build on previous martial arts experience. The particular method, or mix of methods, isn't as important as mastering a "cover and evacuate" rather than a "stay and fight" mindset. **Firearms** The number of armed corporate executive protection details in the United States has grown significantly in recent years. State legislation regarding the use of firearms by protective details varies widely; in any case, training requirements stipulated by any such legislation should be considered as "bare minimum" and not as applicable guidelines for suitable training. It's important to note that executive protection agents' use of firearms is very different from other armed security, law enforcement, or military roles, and armed private sector executive protection agents require a different kind of training than what's required in public sector roles.
Advanced training	Depending on program needs, many types of advanced training might be relevant, for example, various types of tactical firearms training and training for active shooter incidents.

Necessary sustainment training	Repeat conflict management training at least every two years: CQB annually; firearms if and as necessary.

Cyber/Digital Security

Purpose	Protecting the principal and ourselves from cyber/digital vulnerabilities
Basic training	As we and our principals are increasingly online, agents need at least basic training in how to reduce digital risk. This includes secure use of digital tools used by the team (e.g., smartphones, radios, Wi-Fi, VPNs, communication, and other apps including social media), so we ourselves stay safe and don't become vulnerabilities for the principal. It also includes facilitating the safe use of digital tools by the principal, especially while traveling. Unfortunately, training in cyber and digital security is still not a part of most executive protection training schools' basic curriculum.
Advanced training	As necessary according to program needs
Necessary sustainment training	Take refresher courses that update SOPs at least annually.

Security Sweeps

Purpose	Protecting the principal from technical surveillance and remote-controlled devices

Basic training	Many agents receive no basic training in security sweeps at all, but this is changing. Technical surveillance countermeasures (TSCM) is a specialist skill beyond the scope of typical executive protection agents; however, agents should be able to perform basic sweeps and manage vendors. Agents should also understand the basics of sweeps for improvised explosive devices (IEDs) and mail and delivery scanning/searches.
Advanced training	TSCM is constantly evolving along with technological development, so agents with special responsibility for this require more training. Similarly, some agents may need to learn how to handle K9 teams, manage vendors, or require training in explosive ordnance disposal (EOD).
Necessary sustainment training	As necessary according to program needs
Protective Detail Management	
Purpose	Running protective details as effectively and efficiently as possible despite time and other resource constraints. Protective details consist of one or more agents who are either accompanying the principal or preparing to do so via advances, vendor management, or other activities. Common to most all details is that the active agents are on their own, not under the direct supervision of a team lead or manager, and must think for themselves. Protective detail management is an important but often under-appreciated skill set that enables agents to run these details optimally in what are often suboptimal circumstances. Rarely taught in executive protection training schools, mastering these skills can make or break an agent's career.

Basic training	Managing yourself, your team, and your vendors in situations where time and other resources may be scarce: time management and task prioritization; communication; workflow optimization, any applicable legislation or compliance issues; managing the relationship between the protective team and the principal's organization; budgeting and reporting
Advanced training	For those who aspire to or have reached management level, dedicated team lead or team management courses are highly relevant, as could be courses in project management
Necessary sustainment training	As necessary according to agent and program needs

Key Takeaways	
Training is the only way to acquire the 10 capabilities necessary for executive protection	
1	The 10 capabilities for executive protection include: • Conflict management/CQB • Security driving • Medical/hygiene • Cyber/digital • Protective intelligence • Advances & secure travel • Protective detail management • Security sweeps • Escorts • Fixed-site protection
2	Although similar to some of the capabilities required in other security domains (e.g. law enforcement and the military) the 10 protective capabilities are best learned in dedicated courses that prioritize their usefulness in corporate and family office settings.
3	Stakeholders should be aware that each of the 10 protective capabilities may require separate basic, advanced, and sustainment training opportunities.

Chapter 3-4:

Soft skills are hard

In addition to the hard skills outlined in **Chapter 3-3** successful executive protection agents possess a number of other characteristics that can be broadly described as soft skills or personality traits.

In this chapter, we outline the 10 traits that set apart high-performing executive protection agents from the less-great. Many are interrelated; all are important. When an individual agent displays most or all of these traits strongly, they would make a highly successful executive protection agent — and would also do well in many other fields.

The first five traits are particularly significant for the special demands of the protective service industry. Because our over-arching goals are to keep our principals safe and productive no matter where their jobs and other interests take them, we must consistently come up with solutions to new challenges, and we spend a lot of time with principals without being their friends. It requires a certain kind of person to thrive in this context.

The second five traits focus on emotional intelligence (also called EQ), which is also essential for success in corporate EP. Daniel Goleman, who has written extensively on the matter, sums up some key concepts relative to EQ and leadership. We believe these traits apply just as well to EPAs as they do to CEOs.

Resourcefulness

A good EPA needs a special mix of smarts and moxie. We call it resourcefulness. Others might call it problem-solving on steroids: fixing issues and finding solutions — often in new circumstances, usually in time-critical situations.

Executive protection teams are often in situations that are completely new. Changes in venue, tasks, expectations, and many other aspects of the job are commonplace. Even the best SOPs are tested by nonstandard situations. If there's confusion, then the EPA is the one everyone looks to make it all good again.

Resourceful EPAs make do with what they've got and always try to get the best outcome out of any situation. They're creative problem solvers, adaptive, and quick to think on their feet. They ask for what they need — and aren't too shy to ask loudly if that's what's required to get the job done. They always have a Plan B and C. And they never act as if there is anything but Plan A.

The mental habit of thinking ahead is another characteristic of a resourceful EOA, for as Seneca pointed out several thousand years ago, "Luck is what happens when preparation meets opportunity." Good EPAs make their own luck — and deliver superior results — through forward thinking. Their approach resembles that of a chess player more than a checkers fan: They are used to thinking several moves ahead, so they can shape outcomes proactively rather than deal reactively with adverse situations. I believe forward-thinking is so important to quality executive protection that I made it the payoff of my former company. Even when you're two steps behind, you have to be 10 steps ahead.

Resilience

Life is full of stress, and bad things happen — even to good agents. Resilient EPAs aren't the ones who never get into tough situations. We all do that. They're the ones who cope with adversity and keep the mission on track no matter what. Helplessness is never an option.

Psychologically, resilient EPAs are able to navigate through emotional turmoil without turning into a shipwreck. They exude a calm sense of urgency whether everything is business as usual or the situation has leaped into emergency mode. They have the skills and the mindset to counterbalance negative emotions with positive ones. Even when others are succumbing to negativity and pessimism, resilient agents know how and where to dig deep to find more optimism.

Professional Commitment

Commitment to the task of serving the principal is an essential part of executive protection. Ours is, essentially, a service industry.

Good EPAs realize that the security, privacy, and productivity of the principal come first, and the needs of the principal supersede their own needs. They're able to put their personal preferences aside and stand by the client no matter what — before, during, and after the detail. The same extends to the rest of the executive protection team. It's never about you, it's always about the principal.

Successful EPAs also realize this form of professional commitment has nothing to do with the interpersonal commitment that couples promise each other. Professional commitment is a one-way street. It's not reciprocal, and it's not about being the friend of the principal. It's about doing the job we're tasked to do in the most professional way possible.

Discretion

Agents carrying out close protection of a principal are, well, close to the principal. That closeness extends to all kinds of situations that can't be taught at an executive protection school. In addition to protecting principals as they conduct business, agents will often be there when the principal is traveling, enjoying time with family and friends, and just getting on with their life. Complete confidentiality is expected in all matters.

Through it all, good executive protection professionals must maintain their integrity and know their place. Sometimes it's in the foreground and the principal wants to talk; often it's in the background, and the principal has no need to be reminded of their board-mandated, 24/7 protection services.

Discretion can also be seen as loyalty. I've been asked several times why I've never been involved in bodyguard tell-all scandals even though I've worked with a lot of high-profile clients the tabloids would love to sink their teeth into. The answer is simple. When discretion and loyalty are cardinal points on your moral compass — as they invariably are for good agents — what happens in Vegas, stays in Vegas.

Service-Mindedness

Executive protection is a service industry. It's about helping other people (notably, the paying client who has other options) to meet their needs. It's not about you meeting your needs.

If EPAs aren't comfortable working in a job where the needs of the client take precedence over their own, then they should start looking for other work. Because 95 percent of what we do in corporate executive protection is directly related to taking care of the client's requirements for protection, productivity, comfort, and overall well-being. The other 15 percent of the time is spent writing up after-action reviews and expense reports. (Yes, it adds up to more than 100 percent. See the notes on work-life balance below.)

While EPAs might sometimes stay at five-star hotels and eat at three-star Michelin restaurants, they're also the ones who clean up before the principal arrives and make sure there's plenty of the principal's favorite water in the car. They may have even washed the car between bites of a sandwich from a plastic bag.

Some people get the service mentality, others don't. It's not so much about being servile as it is about taking ownership of the job and consistently adapting to the client's needs because that's what the job requires.

Successful EPAs do their jobs, and they help others in the corporate or family office ecosystems to do theirs, too. Because they are service-minded, they know if they make the principal's executive assistant, chief of staff, speech manager, or others look good, then they'll also look good — and the principal will be more likely to be safe and productive.

Self-Awareness

Executive protection professionals must know their strengths as well as their weaknesses. In addition to being clear on their own goals and motivation, they must be able to recognize how their own moods and emotions impact others.

People with a well-developed sense of self-awareness exude self-confidence. They're also able to laugh at themselves and feel no need to over or underestimate their own abilities.

Self-Regulation

Agents need a high degree of self-regulation in order to stay open to change and deal with new or ambiguous situations. Good self-regulation helps them choose their words carefully — and gives them the option of thinking before reacting.

Great EPAs also master another, very particular form of self-regulation. They're able to remain vigilant for hours on end when absolutely nothing is happening. Moment-by-moment situational awareness is key to protection.

Social Skills

Agents must be able to work with people and build relationships to make things happen. The best agents are born networkers who lay the groundwork of solid connections everywhere from the C-suite to the hotel kitchen. They find common ground where others find barriers, and they build good rapport wherever they can.

They're also excellent communicators who get their message across and have the persuasiveness to get their way more often than not. They can read a principal and a situation; they know when it's time to fade into the background or when it's time to engage in conversation; and they understand the difference between assertiveness and aggression.

Empathy

Empathy starts with being aware of other people's feelings and continues by considering their feelings when taking action. For the EPA, these "other people" include not only the principal, but also everyone else in their orbit — and other folks on the executive protection team.

Empathic EPAs thrive in international corporate settings. They pick up on verbal and nonverbal cues that express an individual personality, a corporate culture, and even an entire nation's way of relating and doing business. They recognize the needs of others. And they act accordingly.

But the empathy of good agents is controlled, not unrestrained. Controlled empathy enables the successful EPA to temper warm compassion with cool calculation. We don't drop protocols to please the principal. We recognize how people are feeling, and we acknowledge those feelings through our actions without losing sight of the overall program objectives.

Here, too, good EPAs understand that empathy is not always a two-way street. It's not about us or our feelings; it's about doing the job in the best way possible.

Self-Motivation

This quality is variously called drive, initiative, perseverance, and proactivity. Highly motivated EPAs don't do the job for the money or the recognition. They achieve for the sake of achievement.

A self-motivated executive protection agent is a good executive protection agent. They maintain an optimistic outlook even when the chips are down. A high degree of motivation means the performance bar is always on the way up, and continual improvement is a way of life for the professional executive protection team.

A Different Kind of Work-Life Balance

Corporate executive protection is rarely a nine-to-five job. The client's needs come first, and they can change suddenly.

Balancing the demands of a corporate executive protection work schedule with those of a significant other or young children can be difficult. There's a lot of time on the road, and although the work often seems glamorous and exciting, it can also get lonely. While working, agents are away from home, sometimes at someone else's house with someone else's children. They might get to go to lots of parties, but they're the designated driver every time.

In order to avoid burnout, EPAs need to be brilliant at balancing the demands and perks of the job with all the other parts of their lives. They also need well-managed programs, suitably staffed and led, and career opportunities that allow them to develop and grow.

Key Takeaways

Ten so-called "soft skills" set apart high-performing executive protection agents from the less great

1	The 10 soft skills include: • Resourcefulness • Resilience • Professional commitment • Discretion • Service-mindedness • Self-awareness • Self-regulation • Social skills • Empathy • Self-motivation
2	The first five soft skills apply in particular to agents; the second five are applicable to all.
3	When an individual agent displays most or all of these traits strongly, they'd make a highly successful EPA — and would also do well in many other fields.

Chapter 3-5:

If "training is the cornerstone of readiness," as the US Army writes in *Train to Win in a Complex World* [1], sustainment training is what maintains that readiness over time.

This maxim is equally true in private sector executive protection. Unfortunately, however, the importance of sustainment training in executive protection programs is often neglected. In this chapter, we take a closer look at which executive protection skills need to be maintained through sustainment training — and why sustainment training is too often ignored or underprioritized in executive protection programs.

Some Skills Are Perishable: Use Them or Lose Them

Most of us learned how to ride a bike as children. Acquiring this more or less pure motor skill doesn't come easy and requires lots of trial and error between pedal pushing, falling down, and getting up again. The effort is worth it, however: Once we learn how to keep our balance on a bike, we don't forget — even if years go by between rides.

The brain stores memories — and by extension some skills — in different ways. Bicycle riding, climbing stairs, or the basics of keeping a car on the road all rely on "procedural memory," a kind of long-term memory for motor skills that we perform without being conscious of them. These skills just don't fade away that easily.

Other skills, ones that require different kinds of memory and cognitive processing, are different. If you don't use them, you lose them.

Emergency medicine practitioners, for example, must be proficient in a wide range of procedures to perform competently. Some are simple; others are life-saving and complex. Some are used frequently, others rarely if ever. They are all necessary. High-frequency/low-criticality skills like checking vitals don't perish because they're used all the time. Low-frequency/high-criticality skills like CPR, on the other hand, do fade away if they aren't used.

Who would you want to perform CPR on your loved one — someone who took a course two years ago but hasn't used or retrained the procedure since or someone who does frequent simulation-based training? Research indicates your loved one should prefer the latter[2].

Sustainment Training Keeps Perishable Executive Protection Skills Fresh

Agents need to master a variety of skills, and training in them is a prerequisite for most jobs. Of course, just how much training is required, in what, and at which level, will depend on the program and the position. Everything else being equal, however, it's safe to assume that most agents need at least basic training — and sustainment training — in four key skill areas: medical/ hygiene, driving, defensive tactics, and firearms. Let's take a look at each of these.

Medical/hygiene

Of all the risks that can impact the principal's well-being, medical issues are the most likely to arise. Proficiency in emergency medical procedures, therefore, is arguably the most important skill in the protective toolbox.

The specific proficiencies necessary — and at what level — all depends on the program and its context. In some situations, basic first aid or stop-the-bleed training[3] might be sufficient; other programs might require more advanced skills (such as wilderness EMT certification). In some cases, it could make better sense to add a licensed local physician to the team.

But no matter what the starting point is, sustainment training is necessary to keep medical skills sharp and usable. Best practice would require agents to demonstrate proficiency in their required medical skills at least once a year.

Security driving

Car accidents are another high-probability, high-impact risk. While less likely than dying from heart disease (chance one in six), dying from a motor vehicle crash (chance 1 in 103) is still at the top of the National Safety Council's list of lifetime odds[4], and something that executive protection practitioners must take extremely seriously.

As was the case for medical skills, the skills necessary for security driving depend on the protective program and the context. Not all agents are drivers. Not all executive drivers are EPAs. Some programs require drivers with solid defensive tactics and chauffeur skills only. Others require full-blown evasive and anti-terrorist skills. All would do well to develop and sustain their security awareness[5], understanding of vehicle dynamics[6], and customer service skills[7]. To make things even more complex, when traveling abroad, drivers and vehicles are almost invariably sourced locally.

No matter what the context, given the relative criticality and likelihood of traffic accidents, driver training matters. Unfortunately, a lot of people have a "one-and-done" attitude regarding driver training. In many programs, you're lucky to get recertified every three to five years. In the best of all possible worlds, sustainment training should be mandatory once a year for driving staff. This is easier for executive protection managers to control when dealing with their own employees, but just as important when vetting third-party vendors.

Conflict management/CQB

We need to move beyond all the bullshido and focus on what matters in CQB for executive protection professionals. Realistically, an eight-hour course in Brazilian jiu-jitsu is not going to make you an expert in anything. And even if you've been doing martial arts for a long time, you need to learn what's critical to know within the context of executive protection.

We need to be proficient in some basic stuff that creates time and distance between the principal and trouble — and be gone. Speed, selective aggression, surprise, and techniques that don't steal the show on camera are important. Black belts and advanced skills are nice, but not necessary.

Basic defensive tactics are some of the more perishable executive protection skills and really should be trained a lot more than they are — ideally an hour a week or at least a monthly team session.

The use of firearms doesn't fit into any one-size-fits-all training requirements. Although some programs do use armed agents, most don't. Agents that can carry in the US cannot do so when traveling abroad or even throughout the US; armed EPAs aren't allowed in many countries. So, firearms training wouldn't be important at all in many circumstances.

Where agents are armed, however, everyone would agree they must be trained properly, and sustainment training is important. And that's about where the agreement ends.

Not even police departments within the US have consistent sustainment training standards for the use of firearms. Some require annual training, some semi-annual. Some with a variety of weapons, some with just one. Some experts on firearms training for law enforcement officers recommend relevant, realistic, and regular training, i.e., four times annually. Others would claim this isn't enough.

For armed agents, I recommend mandatory quarterly training as a minimum. I'd also expect agents who are serious about their trade to train on their own once a month to maintain proficiency. If training is done in-house, then it's a good idea to bring in an outside instructor, someone whose good reputation has been carefully vetted, to prevent the team from developing inborn bad habits. There must also be a pass/fail test and agreed procedures for dealing with those who fail their test.

If and when the day comes that the use of firearms is necessary, no training is ever enough. One of the first questions the lawyers will ask will be about training. And they will keep asking.

Why More Clients and Companies Do Not Build in Sustainment Training: Awareness, Time, and Money

Clients, providers, and agents all appreciate the criticality of sustainment training once they become aware of its importance and think through the consequences of having it or not having it. Unfortunately, not everyone is aware of its significance. If there are no incidents that demonstrate the lack of sustainment training — if nothing happens to the principal — then it's easy to remain blissfully unaware of a team's lack of readiness and the poor training standards that contribute to it.

Even if clients and providers do agree on the importance of sustainment training, budget often gets in the way. Who should pay for it: clients, providers, or individual agents? It's far easier to build the costs of sustainment training into SOWs from the beginning than to tack them to ongoing programs later. And it's important to include all the costs — from direct training costs to travel costs — and the cost of replacing team members who are away on training.

Time is perhaps the scarcest resource of all when it comes to sustainment training. To maintain operational continuity, EP managers need to build some redundancy into staffing levels to accommodate time for agent training. Agents need to add time for training to the juggling act of work-life balance. Other, seemingly more important tasks can always get higher priority.

The costs of not prioritizing sustainment training, however, can far outweigh the limited expense of building them into comprehensive executive protection programs. Beyond legal liability, EP programs must also weigh the costs of program failure and client dissatisfaction.

Key Takeaways	
1	Some executive protection skills are perishable: If they aren't used, they'll be lost. These include critical skills within the areas of: • Medical/hygiene • Security driving • Conflict management CQB
2	Perishable skills require sustainment training to keep them fresh and useable if and when needed.
3	Programs fail to provide sustainment training, usually due to unawareness or budget.
4	Even when managers and clients want to provide sustainment training, the lack of staff redundancy necessary to enable operational continuity often gets in the way.

Section 3 Endnotes

1 US Army. *Train to Win in a Complex World*. 2017.

2 American Heart Association. "Frequent simulation-based training may improve CPR proficiency among hospital staff." *Medical Express*, 12 Nov. 2016, medicalxpress.com/news/2016-11-frequent-simulation-based-cpr-proficiency-hospital.html.

3 *Stop the Bleed. EP Access,* epaccess.com/courses/stop-the-bleed/.

4 "Preventable Deaths — Odds of Dying." *Injury Facts*, National Safety Council, 2023, injuryfacts.nsc.org/all-injuries/preventable-death-overview/odds-of-dying/.

5 *Security Awareness: A Systematic Approach to Understanding and Mitigating Driving Risks. EP Access,* https://epaccess.com/courses/executive-security-driving-security-awareness/

6 *Vehicle Dynamics: Applying the Principles of Physics to Your Principal's Safety and Comfort. EP Access,* https://epaccess.com/courses/executive-security-driving-understanding-the-vehicle/

7 *Beyond Chauffeur: The Why and How of Customer Service in Executive Security Driving. EP Access,* https://epaccess.com/courses/executive-security-driving-customer-service/

 SECTION 4:
Managing Changes
in Executive
Protection Programs

Paul was everyone's favorite, until he wasn't.

Paul was a bright young executive protective agent working for a husband-and-wife pair of principals. For her own reasons, the wife thought Paul was the best agent on the team and considered him her favorite agent. Whenever possible, she made sure it was Paul who drove her wherever she needed to go and provided protection for her at public events. This occurred so regularly that both the team and the principal's husband couldn't help but notice.

The husband paid it no mind and was, in fact, supportive and happy that his wife had Paul with her. Paul wasn't experienced enough to realize that he should've downplayed the favorite card instead of pushing it. He began to do everything in his power to make sure he stayed the wife's preferred agent, even if this hurt the team and their overall purpose. For example, he held back information on the wife's preferences, so his fellow agents wouldn't be aware of details such as how she preferred doors to be opened, where to put the gum and mints in the car, and how close she wanted coverage in public. In her mind, the other agents just weren't as competent as Paul. So, after a while, Paul got what he wanted: He was her favorite and went everywhere with her.

Although the rest of the team didn't respect him for playing favorites, he did have the favor of the principals, at least for a while. This, too, changed when the principals' marriage began to unravel.

The husband was unhappy and started engaging in extra-marital activities with a number of women. Things became awkward for the husband when Paul was on coverage. Although the husband liked Paul, it was Paul, after all, who was his wife's favorite. Was Paul more loyal to him or to his wife? Could Paul be counted on to show discretion despite the principal's marital indiscretions?

Paul began to feel the awkwardness, too. He saw what the husband was doing outside the marriage, and although he did his best to remain neutral and keep out of the principal's business, he sensed the husband's waning trust. Things became even more awkward when the wife complained about her marriage to her friends while Paul was standing by on coverage.

The principals eventually took a trial separation, and the wife moved to the beach house. One night shortly after the move, the wife called the command post and Paul answered. She had been trying in vain to reach her husband, but he didn't pick up. "I know he doesn't want to talk to me, but can you please make him take my phone call?"

Ever the favorite, Paul promised to try to accommodate the wife's wishes — knowing full well that the principal was entertaining his mistress and had explicitly asked to not be disturbed. Thinking on his feet, Paul explained the situation to the principal's personal assistant and routed the wife to her, so he could avoid being put in the middle of both principals. The executive assistant handled the situation as the principal wanted, saying he was unavailable, and that she would relay the message to the principal. That was a close call, but Paul thought he had dodged a bullet.

Unfortunately, the marriage continued to disintegrate. When Paul worked with the wife, she'd ask him all kinds of questions about her husband's activities and whereabouts. Whereas Paul had always engaged with her in polite, friendly banter (more than he should have), he now felt the pressure to choose sides. He did his best to stay impartial and not share any information, but this deviated from the previously cozy chattiness he shared with the wife. It was very difficult for Paul to change the dynamic of the relationship from favored agent to neutral outsider. Paul knew he was in trouble.

Once the divorce finally occurred, the security team was split between the husband and the wife, with the husband getting most team members and the wife just a few. Paul was not asked to join the wife's team because she didn't feel close to him anymore, and he stayed on with the husband.

A few months after the divorce the husband decided he didn't want to have Paul around anymore. Every time he saw Paul, it reminded him of his ex-wife. Her favorite agent was no longer a favorite, and he was no longer needed. Paul ended up losing his job because he'd played the favorite instead of playing his cards right. When the family transitioned from married to divorced, he didn't make the transition.

Paul's penchant for playing favorites — facilitated by the principals and his team — led to his downfall after divorce changed the dynamics of the family's protection program. Favoritism is an easy trap to fall into for principals as well as agents. It must be avoided.

Changes are inevitable.

As Benjamin Franklin noted centuries ago, "When you're finished changing, you're finished." For executive protection program managers and other stakeholders, understanding the changes we face at various program pivot points is crucial.

Section 4 examines the key transitions that security programs are likely to face at one time or another. To do so, I borrow from Michael Watkins of IMD, who has written extensively on managing business and career transitions. He provides some actionable insights that can also be applied to the changes that are typical in family security programs. I've tweaked Watkins' five-pointed STARS model[1] down to the four transitions that are most relevant for protection programs:

- **Start-up**
- **Turnaround**
- **Realignment**
- **Sustaining success**

For those tasked with managing security programs, much of Watkins' solid advice holds true across all four transitions. This includes the necessity of aligning program changes with evolving protection strategies, relentless focus on key priorities, and the importance of early wins.

The focus will be on the first two transitional phases — startup and turnaround — as these are the most relevant for most corporations and family offices. I'll then briefly deal with the challenges of realigning a program that, while not currently in distress, will be headed for trouble unless there's a change in course, as well as how to sustain a high-performance program.

The Protective Circle is a helpful tool when considering each of these transitions for the purposes of both planning and diagnostics.

Chapter 4-1:

Starting up an executive protection program

Every protective program starts somewhere. And although many Fortune 500 CEOs and high-net-worth individuals already use protection, a significant segment still doesn't. Navigating the start-up phase of protective programs is particularly tricky for many security directors and would-be principals: They're simply not familiar with executive protection, and they're starting from scratch.

The Transition

This chapter addresses the process of moving from no protection program in place to a working program — even at a small scale. Additions to or expansions of an existing program, e.g., adding a new principal, a new estate, or a new program dimension, can in many ways also be considered as "startups."

Protection programs often evolve from simple to complex, from part-time to full-time. For example, protection may begin with a residential security assessment or secure travel services for an individual principal, then expand to include residential security for one or more residences, and then add additional principals as corporate needs change and families grow. Or, programs might start with residential security only in certain circumstances, such as heightened concerns about persons of interest, then add more coverage, then eventually turn into 24/7 protection.

Similarly, programs can begin with "the basics," e.g., an RTVA that results in part- or full-time:

- Residential security agents
- Secure drivers
- Close protection agents

. . . then evolve to include more "advanced" program dimensions such as:

- Part- or full-time intelligence analysts
- Security operations centers, on- or off-premises
- Event security
- Surveillance detection
- Covert protection

Key Objectives

1. Get a security program running where there has been none.
2. Integrate a new security service into an existing program for the first time.

Key Milestones

1. **Recognition of need:** The principal, family, or CSO decides that a professional security program or additional service is necessary, feasible, and a sound investment, and then selects a provider.
2. **Program design:** The provider defines the processes and the capabilities that will make it happen.
3. **Initial implementation:** Deliver a first impression of operational excellence — even if this is more of a "baby step" than a giant leap forward.

Key Challenges

Lack of experience with professional protection

Most often, principals and family offices new to professional protection have no idea of their relative prominence or how this prominence impacts security, no security expertise, no baseline of "this is how we usually do it," and no opportunity to compare with others. There may be no one on staff with any practical protection insight; often, family offices have no security director, and corporate security departments rarely have track records that include personal protection.

Preconceived notions and misconceptions about protective security abound. Although a security director might have a clear idea about the differences between professional close protection and "bodyguards," the principal and their family may not. Understandably, most principals with no protection experience will easily confuse the tabloid images of intrusive bodyguards with the reality of well-trained close protection agents. They'll quickly pull up the same pictures as the general population: Hollywood stars walking behind a phalanx of muscle-bound men in black, scruff-ups with paparazzi, and insensitive indiscretions with tell-all book deals.

Thus, an important challenge when initiating a protection program for a principal and, possibly, their family, is ignorance of what executive protection actually is (and isn't). Since it's often the case that everyone involved in a new security program will have to reassess their conception of executive protection, one of our most important tasks in the start-up phase is communicating clearly about the actual nature of a professional protective security program and its actual value. The Protective Circle can be particularly helpful at this stage, as it lays out a comprehensive view of good, contemporary executive protection that all stakeholders can understand. It can also be useful in determining how comprehensive the program should be — and which elements should be introduced first.

It's helpful to approach the startup of a new program in an iterative way, where the principal and providers stay in close contact through the initial steps of program initiation in order to dial in the most appropriate program incrementally.

Coordinating with stakeholders

Building corporate and/or family office security networks from scratch requires close teamwork with many parties. Unless the principal is used to professional protection as part of the job, a brand-new protection program will have no established internal network to rely on, so every connection to every stakeholder will have to be created and nurtured. Inclusion of and coordination with all relevant elements of the family office ecosystem, as described above, are essential challenges to be overcome.

A new category of costs

It's essential that corporate and family office accounting managers have a good understanding of what drives costs and who's paying for what. For example, the principal's travel plans changing, as they can from week to week, impacts variable costs due to the advance trips, travel expenses, and agent hours needed to accommodate every new itinerary. So, if the budget was based on 10 trips in a given period, and the principal ends up making more or fewer trips, there will be a discrepancy between planned and actual costs. Does that mean the principals shouldn't take the trips they need to take, or that they should only get security on budgeted trips? Probably not.

Another issue for accountants is making clear distinctions between what a principal's company pays for and what the principal's family office pays for. In theory, it's simple: Business costs are paid by the company; personal costs are paid by the family office. In practice, however, there can be a lot of gray between the black and white rules. Full transparency and proactive dialogue go a long way to prevent problems and address them quickly, if necessary. This applies to those responsible for accounting and to those responsible for running both corporate and personal security programs.

Security program customization

One of the keys to a successful program start is understanding as much as possible about client preferences in order to customize the security program accordingly. Cookie-cutter solutions are rarely sustainable for high-net-worth individuals who are accustomed to arranging the circumstances of their lives according to their wishes rather than simply grabbing a standard solution off the shelf.

To customize client-facing aspects of the security program, a number of guided conversations with the principals and/or their representatives must occur. Covering a range of topics, these conversations can be done in person or in written form and include many areas that the principals and/or their representatives would not consider on their own. The effort is worth it in more ways than one. In addition to gathering important information, the process gets the principal and their families or organizations on your side immediately because they'll see you're covering every base. Some of those conversational topics might include:

- What does the individual or family like or dislike about security? Any pet peeves to understand and work around?
- Should a residential security program attempt to minimize the visibility of security from young children for as long as possible, and present agents as drivers and helpers rather than armed guards? Should covert protection be part of the mix? How should security agents and drivers deal with the things that teenagers do and don't do?

◎ What level of involvement and direct communication between the family and security is appropriate? What is the preferred chain of command? What decisions should the security team make on its own, and what should they seek guidance on?

◎ Are there areas of the estate or residence that are off limits for security? For example, some principals will establish something like a "red zone" (primary bed/bath, private house, etc.) where no staff or security are allowed while they're on property, which turns into a "green zone" when the family goes offsite.

◎ Should we introduce code words and safe phrases, special expressions which, when communicated by the principal or the security team, will convey problems and issues? For example, if the principal is feeling overwhelmed in a crowd looking for photos or autographs, they can say something like, "Can we get a sandwich, please?" so protection agents know the principal has had enough, and the agents need to step in. Something similar can apply if the agents sense there is a problem and want to move the principal to another location.

Hiring new kinds of employees

Few corporate HR departments have experience with protective positions. Family offices may not even have a dedicated HR function. In any case, it's extremely unlikely that organizations new to executive protection have any experience recruiting, developing, and retaining staff within the niche domain of high-end security — or how to build and maintain an effective personal security organization.

Staffing levels must be correct from the start or soon become so. Applying cookie-cutter staffing policies and procedures to family security agents who might be called on to work 80-hour weeks and spend more time on the road than at home will have its own consequences. As seen above, another HR issue is training.

Reporting lines and decision-making authority

In the corporate world, even in convoluted matrix organizations, employees are seldom in doubt as to "who is the boss." Family security is different.

Whereas most CEOs will defer to the chain of command if they notice a lower-level company employee who needs to be nudged, reprimanded, or ultimately replaced, if the principal (or someone in their family) doesn't like a family security protection agent for whatever reason, personal preferences trump organizational hierarchy every time.

The roles and responsibilities of many stakeholders concerned with the principal's security must be understood by all and delineated clearly. As shown in the story of Tom above, there's plenty of room for misunderstanding and friction.

Corporate chief security officers and executive administrative assistants are used to having their say. So are estate managers, family office managers, and security directors. In most cases, however, principals want to deal with one person regarding all aspects of their security programs — not the politics of folks jockeying for positions. Expectations need to be made clear in the beginning.

Important Early Wins

The first 100 days are crucial for corporate and family office security directors. As they get a feel for things and grow into their roles, principals and their families also discover what they do and don't like about the new security program. If the security director's first three months are marred by mishaps and misunderstandings, they're likely to be replaced. Even if the initial period is a success, the tenure of the first security director is likely to last no more than three to five years.

In light of the challenges briefly discussed above, a few initial victories clearly emerge for those who are tasked with starting a family security program from scratch.

Accept the need for personal protection

The first must-win battle is gaining approval from the principal to provide at least some protection services, somewhere, sometime. It often makes good sense to commence a new protection program with "baby steps" rather than a full-blown, 24/7/365 program. This gives everyone involved the opportunity to experience firsthand what professional security actually is. If done properly, it also makes clear that personal security also provides all-important collateral benefits such as improved travel logistics and increased productivity for the principal.

Operational excellence

First impressions matter. Another must-win battle is that of protection quality. It's essential the principal and their respective organizations meet only well-trained and carefully selected protection agents — always, of course, and especially in the early days of the program. While the program might able to survive a less-than-optimal executive protection agent after running for a while, if the principal's and organization's initial perceptions of program quality are negative, it might be too late to fix the reputation of a program that got off to a bad start.

Relationship building

Creating bridges rather than walls between key stake-holders in the corporation, family, estate management, and family office organizations is critical, for without these, the security program will flounder. To build relationships in a start-up program, protection professionals must realize that they have a double role: Not only must they execute their jobs flawlessly, but they must also develop stakeholder understanding of what good protection is and how it happens. This will involve a lot of explaining, and, not least, relentlessly demonstrating a professional approach throughout the corporate and family office ecosystems.

Key Takeaways

There are a range of predictable factors when starting up a new executive protection program:

1	**Key objectives** • Establishing a program where there has been none • Integrating a new service area for the first time
2	**Key milestones** • Recognition of need • Program design • Initial implementation
3	**Key challenges** • Lack of experience with executive protection • Coordinating with stakeholders • The unpredictability of program costs • Customizing protection to individual and family preferences • HR issues, if the program is insourced • Opaque reporting lines in family contexts
4	**Important early wins** • Acceptance of the need for personal protection • Operational excellence • Relationship building

Chapter 4-2:

Considering the many challenges of starting up an executive protection program, it's no wonder that some are more successful than others. Some programs never get off the ground in the first place, while others fail over time. Any number of things can go awry. The wrong people may have been chosen to staff the program. Security managers might engage poorly with agents, the corporate and family ecosystems, or both. There may be no quality control. Complacency might've become the order of the day, resulting in lackadaisical agents.

However, if a protection program isn't performing as expected, that doesn't mean that its underlying objective — the principal's security — is no longer a priority. Rather than simply terminating the program, what's called for is a turnaround.

The Transition

This chapter addresses the process of moving from a dysfunctional or unsatisfactory personal security program to one that works to keep the principals secure and enhance their productivity.

Key Objective

Turn a non-performing protection program into a high-performing program.

Key Milestones

1. Recognition that the personal security program is non-performing
2. Correct assessment of the root cause(s) of the problem(s)
3. Creation of a turnaround plan that prioritizes key issues and improvement steps
4. Focus on early wins

Key Challenges

Awareness

The first hurdle to overcome in a turnaround situation is recognizing the need for change. Moving people beyond denial to realize that there are problems — and that changes are needed to correct these — is imperative. Becoming aware of poorly performing security programs can be difficult for non-professionals, however. If nothing happens to the principal, then it can be tempting to conclude there's nothing wrong with the security. Nothing could be further from the truth.

Lack of ongoing training is one indicator of dysfunction; too much chumminess between family members and security agents is another. But while these and more obvious signs should tip off the casual observer — such as agents who are out of shape physically, sleeping on the job, or whose physical appearance is shabby — determining the technical proficiency of agents isn't something non-professionals can do. Neither is evaluating the appropriateness of agreed-upon SOPs or how well they're followed. This isn't just a question of checking some simple metrics. Those responsible for a poorly functioning personal security program will probably not have a clear way to evaluate success or failure.

A strength, weakness, opportunity, and threat (SWOT) analysis of the program with a focus on problem assessment is essential. The Protective Circle provides a simple diagnostic checklist here. Does the program mitigate risk in a comprehensive way? Are all four of the principal's basic security needs dealt with acceptably? In all contexts? What about the varying categories of threats and vulnerabilities — and agent capabilities?

A SWOT analysis could also include on-site assessments as well as interviews with the principals, security manager and team members, estate, and family office staff. Diagnostic exercises, such as simulating emergency scenarios and asking individual team members what they would do can also be useful: If different agents give different responses, we can assume their SOP and emergency response training leaves something to be desired. It's often more effective to bring in third-party expertise to conduct these analyses rather than to expect that those responsible for creating the situation will also have the wherewithal to rectify it.

Another challenge can be agreeing on the root causes of the problems. It's essential that corporate security directors, principals, and key corporate and family office or estate stakeholders get on the same page before deciding to turn over a new leaf.

Prioritizing the most critical pain points

Since a dysfunctional program may suffer from a long list of troubles, it can be tempting to try to fix all of them at once. This isn't a good idea.

The turnaround process can be compared to medical triage: Among many wounds and illnesses, we have to assign a degree of urgency to all issues, and then tackle them in the optimal sequence. First, stop the bleeding, then start the breathing, protect the wound, and treat for shock.

Identify the roots of the trouble, and then address these aggressively. It's better to hone in on the most critical reasons for the problems affecting the security program and then focus on these relentlessly throughout the turnaround. The turnaround plan should build on solving these few core problems, and early wins should hinge on ameliorating their root causes.

Stabilization

In most cases, the program must go on even while analysis of its problems is taking place: Dropping protection of the principals isn't an option. Stabilizing a program while preparing to change it might bring its own challenges.

Creating a vision for the future

In order to be successful, those responsible for the turnaround must paint a clear picture of how the new personal security program will look once the root causes of underperformance have been identified and corrected. Giving people a realistic image of the light at the end of the tunnel allows them to embrace a shared vision and to look forward rather than backward.

It's important that the vision be clear and compelling, but not so detailed that the turnaround team paints itself into a corner that might be difficult to get out of as the process continues. Creating unrealistic expectations impinges on trustworthiness.

Building credibility

The program's reputation within the corporate and family office ecosystems is all-important, and trust in the protection program is one of the hardest things to rebuild once it's been undermined by poor performance. Therefore, managing expectations through thoughtful communication is essential in all protection program turnarounds.

Transparency around the turnaround process is essential. If there's bad news, then it should all be broken at once rather than rationing it across weeks or months. New teams have the privilege of starting with a fresh slate: They can acknowledge current and past shortcomings, set a new direction, and move on.

Of course, the new team must make good on its promises to build credibility. By communicating achievable goals — and meeting them — security managers build confidence and put precious credit into the emerging program's reliability account.

Important Early Wins

Consensus

Once an analysis is complete, all key stakeholders must be on the same page as to what the core problems are and how the turnaround plan will correct these. Key stakeholders will typically include the principal, CSOs or executive protection managers, estate and/or family office managers, and the family office security manager, if there is one.

Reorganizing for success

If the analysis reveals that there's a person or persons who are standing in the way of a successful program turnaround — or who is/are largely responsible for the program's dismal state — then moving quickly to remove these people from the team is important. This could be one or more security agents and/or their manager. Although it's a difficult thing to do, if the analysis indicates that someone is more part of the problem than of the solution, then they should not be allowed to stand in the way of the turnaround. Furthermore, by reorganizing early on, a signal is sent that there's a willingness to make changes — even the tougher ones.

Reporting using relevant metrics

Since turnaround efforts will rely on metrics that are directly related to the pain points the turnaround is designed to address, it's a good idea to begin reporting against these metrics as soon as possible.

Keeping up Turnaround Momentum

There's a tendency for the people involved in security turnarounds to think that they've completed their jobs once the program is out of immediate trouble. It's natural to celebrate the pain being over, but the festivities shouldn't last too long.

Even though it's easy to overlook or choose not to deal with other underlying issues that might later disrupt the program, smart managers will keep the turnaround going until all concerns have been faced and dealt with. They won't get trapped by the arrogance that their program is so good that it doesn't need any adjustments. They'll root out bad habits and poor results even if they aren't causing immediate pain. They'll be aware of other problems such as favorites syndrome, complacency, and lack of focus on improvement.

Formalized reviews among the principals, security team, corporate, family office, and estate stakeholders are a good way to keep turned-around programs on track and maintain momentum. These should occur at least quarterly, but some relationships require higher frequency to ensure the "unhappiness folder" is kept empty and that the stakeholders feel understood.

Key Takeaways	
There are a range of predictable factors when turning around a failing executive protection program:	
1	**Key objectives** • Turn a non-performing protection program into a high-performing program
2	**Key milestones** • Recognition that the personal security program is non-performing • Correct assessment of the root cause(s) of the problem(s) • Creation of a turnaround plan that prioritizes key issues and improvement steps • Focus on early wins
3	**Key challenges** • Awareness of the need for change • Prioritizing the most critical pain points • Stabilization • Creating a vision for the future • Building credibility
4	**Important early wins** • Creating consensus on the turnaround plan • Reorganizing for success • Reporting using relevant metrics

Chapter 4-3:

Realigning a protective program that needs to change course

Sometimes a security program might seem to be running fine but is actually headed for trouble. Unlike a turnaround situation where the program is clearly in crisis, a program in need of realignment may not be marked by obvious signals of distress or urgency for change.

Another situation that I see sometimes, especially in post-turnaround programs, also indicates that realignments are needed. After having fixed a program's most critical pain points, there's a tendency to think the program is out of trouble and to rest on our laurels. But just because a program's weakest elements have been strengthened doesn't mean the program is as good as it can be. Good managers will continue to push for improvements to make sure the program is always performing at its very best.

The challenges of a realignment transition make up a kind of middle ground between a turnaround and sustaining a successful program. Some program elements work well; others don't. Nonetheless, the careful observer will see clouds gathering on the horizon and realize that if the program sticks to its present course, then significant problems will be inevitable.

If a successful program begins to slip, a realignment could head off the need for a turnaround. If the realignment fails, however, then program turnaround will be the only alternative.

The Transition

Make changes in a program in order to readjust the protective strategy, deliveries, and culture, and thus bolster program quality in the face of current and anticipated challenges.

Key Objectives

Ensure continued program success in spite of predictable factors that will make this more difficult; revitalize a program that's headed for trouble.

Key Milestones

- Building consensus for the need for change
- Realignment plan with concrete steps
- Restructuring as needed

Key Challenges

Complacency

If nothing ever happens to the principal (and fortunately, it rarely does), and they seem fairly happy, then it can be tempting to assume the protection program is performing well. Tempting, but potentially misguided: The program's underlying strategy, culture, and operations might all be in need of an overhaul, and the principal's well-being may well be as much a product of chance as of the protection program's design and execution.

Complacency and the resultant decline in readiness can develop quickly without ongoing quality audits and training. Agents who aren't challenged get bored. Maintaining an alert team that responds to changing risks, needs, and environments requires constant management attention.

Outdated protection strategy

Personal protection strategies need to be critically reviewed from time to time. For one thing, individuals and families change over time. For another, a strategy based on an outdated RTVA isn't as useful as it used to be. Protection strategies that remain unchanged in the face of familial, organizational, technological, or market developments are probably no longer serving their original purpose. The Protective Circle is helpful here, too, as it provides a comprehensive view of executive protection against which the program in question can be compared.

There's no reason to create an entirely new protection strategy every year. But ongoing RTVA updates and periodic strategy audits should inform all realignment processes.

Program culture

Over time, all personal security programs will develop their own culture. A healthy culture will be characterized by attributes such as openness, consistent dedication to improvement, the ability to learn from mistakes, resilience in the face of difficulties, and a high degree of personal accountability — just to mention a few. As for unhealthy cultures, that's the stuff of another book. Entrenched ways of doing things and unspoken rules can be a barrier — as well as a support — to realigning a security program.

Favoritism

One unhealthy executive protection culture is favoritism (as in Paul's story). We all want to be liked, and some of us may be more likable than others in a given situation. But a good protection team doesn't allow favoritism to get in the way of professionalism. As it's been emphasized time and time again, when relationships between some security agents and principals get cozier than others, that's a sure sign of trouble.

Skills gap

A security team that doesn't have the skills it needs to perform at a high level is one thing. This can be addressed by training, new hires, outsourcing, or other means — and indeed often is part of a realignment strategy.

But a security program in need of realignment could well be in the situation where stakeholders simply don't possess the means of properly auditing and rectifying performance.

Important Early Wins

Acknowledging the need for change

The most important early win in a realignment transition is making key stakeholders aware the status quo isn't a sustainable option. This can be difficult to achieve without a burning platform. But unless this new awareness forms the basis of the realignment effort, it will be doomed to fail.

Trust based on shared understanding and expectations

As soon as possible, those responsible for program realignment must focus on building trust between all stakeholders through transparent communication. Describe how a successfully realigned program will look and what's intended to achieve it. Make priorities clear, what we're doing, and why we're doing it. And be sure that all relevant stakeholders understand each other — and feel understood.

Tangible changes in line with the diagnosis

Programs in need of realignment have strengths as well as weaknesses. Managers should aim for clear changes early on that make the strong stronger, and then fix the weaknesses.

Organizationally, this could mean promoting someone who displays the kind of behavior called for by the new strategy, or demoting or removing someone who doesn't prove to be willing or able to do so. In terms of policy, tangible changes could reflect new priorities on readiness and training, advance planning, or practically any other aspect of the program. It all depends on the situation.

	Key Takeaways
	There are a range of predictable factors when realigning an executive protection program that needs to change course:
1	**Key objectives** • Ensure continued program success in spite of predictable factors that will make this more difficult • Revitalize a program headed for trouble.
2	**Key milestones** • Building consensus for the need for change • Realignment plan with concrete steps • Restructuring as needed
3	**Key challenges** • Complacency • Outdated protection strategy • Program culture • Favoritism • Skills gap
4	**Important early wins** • Acknowledging the need for change • Trust based on shared understanding and expectations • Tangible changes in line with the diagnosis

Chapter 4-4:

Sustaining an effective executive protection program

It may seem counterintuitive, but even excellent personal protection programs must be challenged to change in order to stay successful. The best way to do this is to make continuous improvement a cornerstone of the security program and culture.

Unlike the other program transitions described above, changes brought on by continuous improvement efforts are likely to be incremental, not revolutionary. Continuous improvement goals informed by ongoing management follow-up and quality audits should be pursued throughout the program — not only in a few parts of it — and they should be focused on personnel as well as processes and innovation.

The Transition

Incremental transitions, both large and small, come in the form of continuous adjustments and improvements to the security program. Smaller adjustments could include tweaking SOPs and KPI alignment. Larger adjustments might be changes in personnel or providers.

Key Objectives

Keep a high-performing executive protection program on track — and make it even better.

Key Milestones

- Road map to structure all continuous improvement processes
- Creating and using clear metrics, both qualitative and quantitative, that are consistently measured relative to a baseline to determine progress or lack thereof. These metrics should be clearly understood by all stakeholders and enable evaluation of both "hard" and "soft" issues, from tactical execution to alignment with the principals' preferences.

Key Challenges

Developing a high-performance culture

Personal security programs with high-performance cultures are easy to recognize but hard to copy. High-performance teams and organizations have cultures to match and often share a number of characteristics. These include:

- Excellent leadership aligned with the overall organization
- Lean organizational structure with clear roles and responsibilities
- Ongoing motivation of the organization's engagement in excellence and readiness to change, including a dedication to continuous learning as individuals and as a team
- A strong HR strategy that focuses on recruiting the very best talent for every role, and then developing it even further

Comparative analysis and benchmarking

It's always possible to learn from the best in the field, and benchmarking a program with high performers is an excellent way to do it.

Within the specialized niche of executive protection, however, this isn't as easy to do as in other areas. One way is to network and compare notes with other directors of security and executive protection managers; another is to hire a third-party provider with a proven track record of excellence in family security to perform a comparative review.

Important Ongoing Wins

The wins we want in sustaining successful programs are continuous and will typically be baked into the program itself. Remember, success breeds success . . . until it doesn't. Never get complacent!

No matter what transition is next for an executive protection program, one thing is sure: We're never better than our last detail. So, step up and never step down. Constant focus on quality deliveries should always be an objective for the entire team as they rise above self-limiting behavior to meet the ever-changing challenges of best-in-class security.

Key Takeaways	
There are a range of predictable factors when sustaining an effective executive protection program:	
1	**Key objectives** • Keep a high-performing executive protection program on track — and make it even better
2	**Key milestones** • Road map to structure all continuous improvement processes • Creating and using clear metrics, both qualitative and quantitative
3	**Key challenges** • Developing a high-performance culture • Comparative analysis and benchmarking

Section 4 Endnotes

1 Watkins, Michael D. *The First 90 Days: Proven Strategies for Getting Up to Speed Faster and Smarter*. Expanded ed., Harvard Business Review Press, 2013.

WRAP UP & RESOURCES

Afterword:

The executive protection industry has grown significantly since I joined it more than three decades ago. But has the practice itself evolved just as appreciably over the same time span? Yes and no.

On the one hand, the business of executive protection has clearly undergone some very noticeable changes. For one thing, there's more of it: There are more principals getting protection, more programs, and more agents working than ever — and all the industry insiders I talk to believe this upward trajectory will only continue throughout the foreseeable future. For another, there's already been a good amount of consolidation — the biggest players have gotten bigger through a wave of mergers and acquisitions, especially over the past five to 10 years — and plenty more deals are sure to come as bigger fish gobble up smaller fish, only to be eaten themselves by some very big fish. To be fair, it's also true the industry has undergone some professionalization over the past few decades. There are more and better training options; best practices are increasingly shared, if only informally, as practitioners gain experience in and move between different programs and different companies; and there are serious efforts now taking place to create national standards for executive protection.

Conversely, however, not much has changed at the level of operations and tactical execution. Distinguishing quality executive protection from "security theater" is still too difficult for most. Too many EP schools still teach the same tired old lessons they did 20 years ago. Despite oceans of ink dedicated to the coming "convergence" of digital and physical security, far too few executive protection programs can be considered technically savvy: they neither protect their principals (or themselves) adequately from digital threats, nor do they sufficiently use tech to deliver better quality at a lower cost, as has been done successfully, and disruptively, in many other industries.

What Future Changes Can We Expect?

The foundations of good executive protection described in *The Protective Circle* were valid when I wrote my first book, and I'm convinced that most of them will also be useful in the future. The basic principles of personal risk management most likely won't change so fast. However, I do believe that the industry will see at least two significant shifts in the near future in how these principles are applied.

The first shift will be a growing focus on quality management systems. Quality in executive protection operations is still too much of a black box. One of the primary challenges in assessing the quality of what we do is the intangible nature of our service. Unlike physical products, protection services are experienced in real-time, making it difficult for clients (and even many providers) to objectively evaluate the efficacy of the measures in place. Moreover, and importantly, the absence of any security incidents or threats doesn't necessarily indicate that the quality of protection is adequate. It's crucial to recognize the quality of an executive protection program might be abysmal even if nothing happens to the principal and the client happily pays for it year after year.

By implementing better quality management in everything (e.g., comprehensive risk assessments, proactive planning) agent training, vendor management, and transparent client communication — the best executive protection companies, whether big or small, will help clients and colleagues to differentiate effective risk mitigation from mere "security theater" and push the industry in a positive direction.

The second shift will be a greater focus on innovation. I'm not sure when or if the executive protection industry will experience the equivalent of what Airbnb did to the hotel industry, but I'm sure it could happen.

I believe we can expect to see incremental innovation coming from the major providers, who will continue to try to improve their services for their biggest, most demanding, and often most profitable customers, but this is probably not where the most disruptive innovation will occur. When things could really get interesting is if a newcomer uses a new twist on technology to go for segments the major incumbents don't prioritize, e.g., less profitable or underserved customers, to provide a solid service for a lower cost — and then work their way up to eat the incumbents' lunch. It has happened in other industries. Remember when Blockbuster had retail outlets everywhere renting millions of VHS tapes and Netflix was mailing DVDs to a very small niche?

What will AI and ever better, cheaper cameras and sensors mean for manned residential security programs? Where is the garage startup working on the secure travel service that's as safe or safer than what many EP companies can provide, as easy to use as Uber, and cheaper than a limo company?

If you're also interested in the future of executive protection, please stay in touch. Feel free to ping me via social media, check out my new blog, or say hello at an industry event.

Best regards,

Christian West

@danishvikingcw
cw@christian-west.com
www.christian-west.com
www.linkedin.com/in/christianwest1/

Glossary

The Protective Circle — a model that explains the importance of holistic thinking regarding not only our principals' varies security needs, but also the multiple categories they typically face — and the protective capabilities required to mitigate the resulting risks

- **BOLO** — Be on the lookout
- **CQB** — Close-quarters battle
- **CRO** — Chief risk officer
- **CSO** — Cheif security officer
- **EA/EAA** — Executive assistant/Executive administrative assistant
- **EOD** — Explosive ordnance disposal
- **EP** — Executive protection
- **EPA** — Executive protection agent
- **EQ** — Emotional intelligence
- **Fixed sites** — places where our principals spend solid chunks of time in one spot, regularly or irregularly (residences, offices, hotels, etc.)
- **GOI** — Group of interest
- **GSOC** — Global security operations center
- **HR** — Human resources
- **IED** — Improvised explosive device
- **KPI** — Key performance indicator
- **Organigram** — organizational chart
- **POI** — Person of interest
- **PR** — Public Relations

- **RFP** — Requests for proposals
- **Risks** — the potential for harm (loss, damage, etc.) to the principal that arise when threats exploit or circumvent vulnerabilities.
- **RTVA** — Risk, threat, and vulnerability assessment
- **SOC** — Security operations center
- **SOP** — Standard operating procedure
- **SWOT**— Strength, weakness, opportunity, and threat
- **Threats** — the bad things (and/or people, events, circumstances, etc.) that might or could cause harm to the principal
- **TSCM** — Technical surveillance counter measures
- **Vulnerabilities** — weaknesses in protective programs — or gaps in the Protective Circle — that can be exploited or otherwise surpassed, so threats can reach and harm the principal.

About the Author

Christian West is an executive protection architect and entrepreneur with decades of international experience. He has successfully founded, led, and sold two leading executive protection companies, AS Solution and West Security. A sought-after speaker, EP trainer, and security advisor in Europe and the United States, Christian is an active blogger who has written dozens of blogs and two bestselling books on executive protection. Christian founded Asgaard Technologies to bring to market ProtectionManager, the world's first app suite designed exclusively for the executive protection industry. He is also an advisor in several security technology companies. Christian founded EP Access in 2021 to provide high-quality training for EP professionals.

Printed in the USA
CPSIA information can be obtained
at www.ICGtesting.com
JSHW011937180924
69977JS00002B/4